# Perceived Control, Motivation, & Coping

# Sage Series on Individual Differences and Development

### Robert Plomin, *Series Editor*

The purpose of the **Sage Series on Individual Differences and Development** is to provide a forum for a new wave of research that focuses on individual differences in behavioral development.

## Editorial Board

## Books in This Series

# Perceived Control, Motivation, & Coping

## Ellen A. Skinner

**Individual Differences and Development Series**
**VOLUME 8**

**SAGE** Publications
*International Educational and Professional Publisher*
Thousand Oaks   London   New Delhi

*For information address*:

SAGE Publications, Inc.
2455 Teller Road
Thousand Oaks, California 91320

SAGE Publications Ltd.
6 Bonhill Street
London EC2A 4PU
United Kingdom

SAGE Publications India Pvt. Ltd.
M-32 Market
Greater Kailash I
New Delhi 110 048 India

Printed in the United States of America

**Library of Congress Cataloging-in-Publication Data**

Skinner, Ellen A.
 Perceived control, motivation, and coping
/ Ellen A. Skinner.
  p. cm. — (Sage series on individual differences and
development; vol. 8)
  Includes bibliographical references and index.
  ISBN 0-8039-5560-X. — ISBN 0-8039-5561-8 (pbk.)
  1. Control (Psychology) 2. Motivation (Psychology)  I. Title.
II. Series.
BF611.S56   1995
155.2'4—dc20                                    94-23859

95  96  97  98  99  10  9  8  7  6  5  4  3  2  1

Sage Project Editor: Susan McElroy

This book is dedicated to my mentors. In chronological order of their appearance: Marjorie Wilkinson Skinner, Gordon B. Skinner, Larry Kurdek, Richard M. Lerner, Paul B. Baltes, and Edward L. Deci.

*"Spinoza said the eyes of the mind are proofs, but Noam regards proofs more in the way of spectacles, bringing the visions of intuition into sharper focus."*

Rebecca Goldstein (1983, p. 47)
*The Mind-Body Problem*

# Contents

# Series Editor's Preface

I am pleased to welcome Ellen Skinner's book to the **Sage Series on Individual Differences and Development**. The Series includes explorations, from the perspective of individual differences, of several areas of developmental research: environmental influences (Wachs, Plomin), young children's close relationships (Dunn), personality (Loehlin), infant cognition (Colombo), childhood language (Shore), and underachievement at school (McCall). In this book, Ellen Skinner tackles one of the most important, and most difficult, areas of developmental research. The general topic is naive causal models of control, which encompasses a wide range of constructs of control such as self-efficacy, learned helplessness, locus of control, and attribution. Perceived control has been the focus of Ellen Skinner's research and she brings to this book her characteristically thoughtful and careful approach that tames this sprawling area. What I like best is the energy, enthusiasm, and clarity that shines through the book. In an area that seems to lend itself to pedantic and dreary obfuscation, Ellen Skinner's vigorous, engaging, and no-nonsense writing style is especially stimulating. Just read the introduction and you will be hooked.

It is a safe prediction that Ellen Skinner's book will become both a milestone of current research and a map for future research on perceived control. The future lies in the investigation of the mechanisms and limits of control in new domains, in interventions, and in development. But this is not just a specialty book. In the long run, the most valuable feature of the book is its breadth. Ellen Skinner shows how perceived control goes far beyond cognitive appraisal and engages some of the key issues in development. The book focuses on the motivational and coping links between belief systems and success or failure, and also considers the interface between perceived control and emotion, attachment, child-rearing, and education. No matter what your area of expertise, the book will stimulate your thinking. For example, the book convinced me that perceived control is a core aspect of children's active construction of their experiences. The legacy of the book will be to lead to the use of constructs of perceived control in research in these other areas—the penultimate chapter is a valuable how-to prescription (and how-not-to proscription) for accomplishing this.

ROBERT PLOMIN

# Acknowledgments

It is a pleasure to acknowledge the many contributions of colleagues and students to my research and thinking. Many experts in the control field have provided instructive feedback, including Margret Baltes, Albert Bandura, Jochen Brandstaedter, Bert Brim, Jr., Virginia Crandall, Carol Dweck, Heinz Heckhausen, Walter Mischel, Martin Seligman, Bernard Weiner, and John Weisz. I have been very lucky with colleagues, including my collaborators at the Max Planck Institute—Paul Baltes, Michael Chapman, and Bernhard Schmitz—as well as my other German colleagues Rainer Reisenzein and Manfred Schmitt. I am pleased that research on the construct of control continues successfully at the Institute with Jutta Heckhausen, Todd Little, Gabriele Oettingen, and Anna Stetsenko. Work with the Motivation Research Group at the University of Rochester is always fun and thought-provoking, and for that I thank Edward Deci and Richard Ryan. Special appreciation is reserved for James Connell and James Wellborn, whose insight and enthusiasm have made them valued collaborators over many years.

My research teams of postdoctoral, graduate, undergraduate, and staff members have been delightful and productive. They include the Berlin group, Werner Grezeck, Birgit Herbeck, Jane Johnson, Ulman Lindenberger, Richard Newman, Anita Schindler,

Christa Schmidt, and Martin Teschechne; the Rochester group, Jeff Altman, Michael Belmont, Helen Dorsett, Jennifer Herman, Marianne Miserandino, Brian Patrick, Cara Regan, and Hayley Sherwood; and the new Portland group, Cathleen Edge, Sandy Grossmann, Ron Yoder, and Melanie Zimmer-Gembeck. Special recognition goes to Peter Usinger, whose work spanned all three research teams.

I express my deep appreciation to the W. T. Grant Foundation, to its past President Robert Haggerty, and its current President Beatrix Hamburg and Vice President Lonnie Sherrod, whose support through a Faculty Scholar Award provided the time to complete this book. I am also happy to acknowledge support from Research Grant No. HD19914 from the National Institute of Child Health and Human Development, and Training Grant No. 527594 from the National Institutes of Mental Health, as well local support from Portland State University.

In the production of the book, I would like to thank reviewers Judy Dunn, Jutta Heckhausen, Thomas Kindermann, and Gordon Skinner, as well as an anonymous reviewer, for their considered comments on earlier drafts; I especially thank series editor Robert Plomin. I also thank James Wellborn for his creative and conceptual contributions to the graphics, and Sandy Grossmann for her editorial work.

No one finds the time to write a book without taking time away from other important commitments. And so I would like to thank my family, Marjorie and Gordon Skinner, Laura and Larry Webb, and Leona and Thomas Kindermann, for their unflagging encouragement during this interesting process.

# Introduction

The images created by reading the research on perceived control are vivid and visceral. Seligman's dogs are huddled in a corner, fearfully awaiting painful shocks, even though with one leap over the barrier, they could escape. Watson's tiny infants are lying on their backs, kicking their feet and cooing joyfully as they turn the mobiles over their heads. One of Dweck's children is talking aloud as he experiences repeated failures; he is ruminating about how badly he did on the last problem and what he will be having for lunch. Another of Dweck's children hitches his chair up to the table, rubs his hands together, saying, "*Now* this is starting to get interesting!"

Averill's college student is looking at the button on the side of his chair and deciding to take another blast of painfully loud noise before terminating the experiment. Bandura's heart attack victims are wondering if they are capable of following through on the exercise program prescribed by their doctors. Langer and Rodin's old people are sitting in the recreation room of their institutional home, listening to the director encouraging them to decide what to eat, what movies to watch, and giving them a plant for which they will be responsible. They don't know it yet, but they will live longer than their counterparts on another floor of the same institution who do not participate in this intervention.

The research on perceived control is a scrapbook of images that span the domains of human functioning as well as the life course. Experiences of control have enriched everyone's lives. And, inevitably, loss of control visits everyone as well: failure, divorce, illness, aging, loss of loved ones. At certain social addresses and historical times, the impact of powerful and chaotic forces is more apparent. What people have in common across historical time, social status, and age, however, is the need for control. In the words of Gurin and Brim (1984), "The sense of control, inextricably linked developmentally to beliefs about causation, is fundamental to human life" (p. 282).

## Purpose of the Book

This book is written for all the colleagues and students who, over the years, have called or written for advice on perceived control. These are the more precise answers I wish I had given over the telephone and the long-winded explanations I wish I had been able to include in letters. I have tried to answer basic questions about the nature and components of perceived control. I have tried to speak to the critics of perceived control, explaining the limitations of the construct, and I have tried to address its potential friends, describing how to decide whether to include perceived control in a program of research. I have written about my own ideas without detailing the decades of work on the topic that preceded them, but I hope that my respect for that work is apparent.

I discovered the topic of perceived control while pursuing my interest in the development of enthusiasm. One of the most appealing characteristics of young children is their ceaseless unbounded curiosity about how the world works. And one of the saddest developments is the emergence of individual differences in which some children maintain their enthusiasm, optimism, and interest while others become anxious, fearful, and withdrawn in the face of challenges. The development of these individual differences led me to the construct of perceived control, as a powerful mechanism underlying their emergence. The study of perceived control is located at the interface of many areas in sociology and psychology, including social, personality, clinical, health, educational, organizational, sports, and developmental; it touches many other broad topics, such as motivation, social cognition, coping, and the self; and it plays a role in development from infancy to old age. No one can be an expert on all these areas, but it may be useful to analyze some of the general themes that continue to surface across them. I have tried to bring enthusiasm to the task.

## Overview of the Book

This book is divided into seven sections, arranged from the most fundamental to the most complex issues. *Part I* summarizes the *meta-theoretical basis* for a needs theory of perceived control. *Part II* briefly sketches the place of other theories within this model and presents a *new conceptualization* of perceived control. *Part III* covers the *antecedents* of perceived control, looking at the emergence of a sense of control in social interactions as well as contextual features that promote and undermine control. *Part IV* focuses on the *consequences* of control, specifically on motivation and coping. *Part V* details the *development* of control, largely unexplored territory, especially issues of developmental change in the mechanisms by which control is constructed and expressed. *Part VI* describes the implications for *interventions* into the competence system, highlighting gaps in knowledge that make it difficult to optimize perceived control in children, adults, and the elderly. Finally, *Part VII* outlines the questions researchers will ask themselves as they decide whether to use control constructs in their research, and suggests an *agenda* for future study of development and individual differences.

## Overview of the Theory

In the broadest sense, perceptions of control can be thought of as naive causal models individuals hold about how the world works: about the likely causes of desired and undesired events, about their own role in successes and failures, about the responsiveness of other people, institutions, and social systems. As noted by Brim (1976), it can be thought of as a "self-theory": "One's sense of personal control is in fact a system of belief, i.e., a theory about oneself in relation to one's environment, and a concern with causality, whether outcomes are a consequence of one's own behavior or tend to occur independently of that behavior" (p. 243).

People strive to experience control because humans have an innate need to be effective in interactions with the environment. The experience of control is joyful, the loss of control can be devastating. Individual's interpretations of these experiences are reflected cumulatively in their control beliefs, which constitute a major self-system process. The innate universal need gives power to people's beliefs. Beliefs about control do not consist of cold procedural knowledge about causes and effects; they are hot potent constructions, imbued with emotion and personal significance.

Perceptions of control influence whether responses are initiated; have an impact on emotional reactions to success and failure; influence how well intentions can be implemented; and promote or impede effort, exertion, and persistence. They are particularly critical in times of stress. Perceived control influences whether people actively test hypotheses and strategies, seek information, and plan, or instead lapse into passivity, confusion, avoidance, rumination, and anxiety. Collectively, these outcomes are referred to as *action* and *action regulation*, and they are typically studied as motivation and coping. They in turn underlie success and failure many life tasks and domains.

Perceived control is shaped by development and is an active force in guiding development as well. Individuals who believe they have control act in ways that make success more likely and so confirm their initial high expectations of control. Furthermore, their sustained engagement in challenging tasks is likely to lead to the development of actual competence over time. In contrast, individuals who do not believe they can influence outcomes act in ways that forfeit opportunities for exerting control. Over time, through their passivity and avoidance of difficult tasks, they forgo the development of new competencies. Individual differences in developmental trajectories of both subjective control and objective competence will result.

Although research documents that individual differences in control are important across the life span, development changes how they are organized and how they function. The experiences that contribute to a sense of control change with age, as does the causal reasoning that interprets experiences into beliefs. Developmental change is seen in the very nature of the self to which control is attributed. Changes are also evident in the other causal categories used to explain control experiences, like ability, chance, and luck. Age, as well as gender, class, and race, influence actual opportunities and limitations for control as well as how the social context interprets an individual's successes and failures.

The core themes of the book reflect an attempt to explore the complex interplay between person, context, and development as they shape individual differences in perceived control. The challenge of bringing together developmental and individual differences perspectives is twofold: to discover how individual differences in developmental trajectories are created and maintained or deflected; and to discover how normative developmental changes affect the way children and adults construct and express individual differences in perceived control. Bringing together the sometimes seemingly disparate work on individual differences and developmental change in perceived control has the potential to enrich both areas of study.

# PART I

# Meta-Theoretical Assumptions

# 1

# What Is Perceived Control?

*Somewhere between the conditions of slavery and omnipotence the mass of humanity lives out ordinary lives, each person seeking to master his or her part of the world, and in the course of this developing beliefs about how it works, and who, or what controls the events of life.*

Orville G. Brim, Jr. (1974, p. 1)

Perceived control is a powerful construct. Five decades of research have established it as a robust predictor of people's behavior, emotion, motivation, performance, and success and failure in many domains of life (for reviews see Baltes & Baltes, 1986; Brim, 1974; H. Heckhausen, 1991; Lefcourt, 1981, 1983; Peterson, 1980; Strickland, 1989). Perceived control consistently predicts behaviors as diverse as adherence to medical regimes and winning baseball games. Reviews consider its relation to health, achievement, school performance and retention, motivation, interpersonal competence, political beliefs, social action, parenting, teaching, marital satisfaction, work success, conformity, creativity, problem-solving, information seeking and processing, emotion, and longevity. In clinical work, control has been implicated in coping, depression, anxiety, alienation, apathy, phobias, self-esteem, and personal adjustment to critical life events.

In research on stress, loss of control is one of the few forms of psychological trauma that researchers can agree is universally aversive. Competence and control are major themes in discussions of the self (Harter, 1983). Four influential theories of perceived control

3

have guided thinking in this area; they are centered on the constructs of locus of control (Lefcourt, 1981), causal attributions (Weiner, 1985a, 1986), learned helplessness (Seligman, 1975), and self-efficacy (Bandura, 1977, 1986). These theories continue to generate hundreds of studies each year, and are the basis for interventions in families, businesses, hospitals, marriages, nursing homes, workplaces, classrooms, and therapists' offices.

## Misperceptions About Perceptions of Control

As a result of its empirical success, perceived control is a familiar construct to most psychologists. Unfortunately, it is easier to be familiar with stereotypes about perceived control than with current conceptions (Lefcourt, 1992; Rotter, 1975). Because many of these stereotypes refer to the fundamental nature of perceived control, dispelling them is a good place to start.

*A Set of Beliefs Versus a Trait.*   Perceived control is often thought of as a personality construct. Because locus of control scales are used to identify individual differences, it is easy to assume that an individual's generalized sense of control constitutes a stable, enduring, cross-situational trait-like predisposition (cf. Rotter, 1990); studies in which individuals are labeled as "internals" and "externals" contribute to this impression. In current conceptualizations, however, perceived control is usually considered a flexible set of interrelated beliefs that are organized around interpretations of prior interactions in specific domains. In contrast to personality traits, these belief sets are viewed as constructed by individuals; hence, they are open to new experiences and can be altered.

*Based on a History of Experiences Versus Situational Information*   If perceived control is *not* a personality construct then it is tempting to conclude that it must be a fleeting situation-specific perception. Given their power in regulating behavior and affect, it would indeed be convenient if beliefs could be changed easily, for example, through verbal persuasion or a few disconfirming experiences.

However, perceived control can be remarkably tenacious and, on occasion, intractable.

Perceptions of control are constructed from an individual's history of experiences interacting with the social and physical context. In some domains, such as with parents, teachers, or spouses, these experiences number in the hundreds of thousands and take place over decades. Hence, beliefs about control are not just ideas; they are phenomenologically "real." They are convictions about how the world works. A great deal of contradictory evidence would be required to alter them. However, individuals are unlikely to encounter experiences that disconfirm their beliefs in the normal course of events, simply because the way individuals interact with the environment is based in part on their beliefs about control.

*Part of a System Versus a Single Construct.* Sometimes it seems that beliefs about control are most easily thought about as measurement instruments, that is, as isolated sets of beliefs. When considering whether to include a construct in a particular study, the decision is often based on how many studies showed or failed to show a connection between the corresponding measure and a target variable. Of course, perceived control is not just an isolated construct or a single measure. In each of its formulations, it is part of a larger system. In expectancy-value theories, control interacts with incentive value to predict behavior; in diathesis-stress models, perceived control only operates in conjunction with negative life events; in volitional theories, perceived control is part of a sequence of action control. Theory is needed to make even the simplest decisions: which sets of beliefs to assess, whether they should be domain specific or general, whether they are developmentally appropriate, and, of course, whether and why they should be related to the phenomenon of interest.

## Challenges to the Study of Perceived Control

Because this book is being written during an era in which the self and cognitive constructs are once again legitimate topics of study, it is unlikely that anyone would question whether a person's *beliefs* can actually have any kind of impact on his or her functioning and development. However, this was not always the case. Several formulations of perceived control became prominent while behaviorism was still a powerful meta-theory, and serious challenges were leveled against them. Even now, it is instructive to examine how these charges were empirically rebutted, and, perhaps more important, to consider their potential validity. Given its current popularity as a construct, perhaps it is even more important today to acknowledge the real challenges to the study of perceived control.

*Epiphenomenon.* The most serious charge against perceived control is that it is an epiphenomenon. The argument holds that, although correlations do exist between perceived control and many outcomes, these relationships are spurious: Both control beliefs and outcomes were caused by a third variable. Many good candidates for third variables exist. For example, in correlating self-efficacy with subsequent behavior, critics argued that previous behavior predicted both: People who succeed will have high self-efficacy and they will continue to succeed. Bandura was able to show that self-efficacy predicted future behavior, over and above the effects of past behavior (Bandura, 1977).

Another good candidate is actual competence. For example, critics argued that the correlations between perceived control and academic performance are due to intelligence: Smart kids have higher perceived control and do better in school. Researchers were able to demonstrate that perceived control actually accounts for more variance in school grades and achievement test scores after controlling for intelligence (Schmitz & Skinner, 1993; Stipek & Weisz, 1981). Perceived control is most closely related to the part of school grades that is due to effort and persistence, and *not* to the part due to ability.

Empirical data can ward off specific claims, but they do not alter the basic premise. Perceived control is influenced by previous behavior and previous successes and failures. And so, any *consequence* of perceived control could also in principle be influenced by the same antecedents that produced the feeling of control. This possibility is an alternative hypothesis in any study examining the effects of perceived control.

*Reciprocal Relations.* Another alternative interpretation for relations between perceived control and performance is reciprocal effects. Relations are likely to be a product of both the effects of control on performance and the effects of performance on control. Extremely high correlations, which are often the case in achievement domains, probably include estimates of relations in both directions. Research using experimental and time-lagged designs has shown that perceived control does influence subsequent performance. But such research has also demonstrated that success and failure also have effects on subsequent control beliefs (Lachman, 1986b; Schmitz & Skinner, 1993; Stipek, 1980).

*Perceived Control as a Life-Span Phenomenon.* Ironically, the greatest challenge in the study of perceived control is created, not by the weaknesses of the construct, but by its extraordinary success. The challenge is to use everything that has already been discovered about the nature and functioning of the competence system. Hundreds of studies each year include control-related constructs. The literature is replete with innovations in conceptualizations of control, new measures, analyses of new domains and age groups, identification of antecedent conditions, interventions to increase control, and discoveries of new classes of mechanisms that mediate its effects. Participants in these studies are college students, cancer patients, elementary school-aged children, rape survivors, elderly residents of nursing homes, representative samples of middle-aged adults, adolescents whose parents are divorcing, and neonates. Studies examine how people of all ages exercise control, search for control, find control, take control, relinquish control, regain control, delude themselves about control, and accommodate to losses of control. The challenge for researchers in this area is to form a coherent picture of how the competence system functions in their target domain and age group that nevertheless allows them to selectively incorporate the most important of the new discoveries from other areas and developmental periods.

# 2

# What Is the Need
# for Competence?

Why are perceptions of control so important to psychological functioning? Why are they connected to such positive emotions, like joy and enthusiasm, but also to such intense negative ones, like fear and depression? Why aren't perceptions of control simply cold cognitions, akin to causal reasoning? Why is loss of control such a devastating experience, resulting, in some species, even in death? Why are the effects of perceived control so widespread, seen across domains of life and across the life span? One answer can be framed using a meta-theoretical assumption: Perceived control reflects the fundamental human need for competence.

From this perspective, all humans come with an inborn desire to interact effectively with the environment and so to experience themselves as competent in producing desired and preventing undesired events. All people need to experience control. The need for competence, or effectance, is considered innate and universal, a part of human nature (Connell, 1991; Connell & Wellborn, 1991; DeCharms, 1968; Deci, 1975; Deci & Ryan, 1985; Harter, 1978; Koestner & McClelland, 1990; White, 1959). As DeCharms (1968) states, "man's primary motivational propensity is to be effective in producing changes in his environment. Man strives to be a causal agent. His nature commits him to this path and his very life depends on it" (p. 269).

The definitive argument for this kind of motivation was made by White in 1959, in his classic paper, "Motivation Reconsidered: The Concept of Competence." White wove together empirical and conceptual arguments from a wide range of perspectives to support the proposition that humans are intrinsically motivated to create effects on their environments. From behaviorism, he quotes Zimbardo and Miller on the reinforcement value of "effect[ing] a stimulus change in the environment" (White, 1959, p. 302). From psychoanalytic theory, he cites Hendrick's notion that all people have "an inborn drive to do and to learn how to do" (p. 307). Seen as the basis for mastery, exploration, manipulation, and the search for excitement and stimulation, the behavior motivated by effectance is "directed, selective, and persistent, and it is continued not because it serves primary drives, . . . but because it satisfies an intrinsic need to deal with the environment" (White, 1959, p. 318). Effectance motivation results in active goal-directed engagement, and because responses must be adapted in order to produce effects, it eventually influences development. "To the extent that these results are preserved by learning, they build an increased competence in dealing with the environment. The child's play can thus be viewed as serious business, though to him it is merely something that is interesting and fun to do" (White, 1959, p. 321).

The roots of effectance motivation are seen as genetic and serve an evolutionary function. White (1959) cites B. F. Skinner, "We may plausibly argue that a capacity to be reinforced by any feedback from the environment would be biologically advantageous, since it would prepare the organism to manipulate the environment successfully before a given state of deprivation developed" (p. 316). Individuals who dedicate time and energy to figuring out how to operate the contingencies in their environment, and who actually enjoy this process, will learn a great deal about effective and ineffective strategies, about their own capacities, and about the limitations inherent in themselves and the context.

"In spite of its sober biological purpose," writes White, "effectance motivation shows itself most unambiguously in the playful and investigatory behavior of animals and young children" (p. 329). Effectance motivation is reflected in experimental analyses of animal behavior, as well as in naturalistic observations of children's play, in which the image described by Groos in 1901 of a child running toward a mud puddle in order to plant a mighty splash, is familiar to all parents. In support of his proposition, White (1959) cites Groos: "we demand a knowledge of effects and to be ourselves the producers of effects" (p. 316). The theme is also apparent in Piaget's (1976, 1978) descriptions of cognitive development and its activities in infancy, as 3-month old Laurent works busily at a string attached to a rattle, to "make interesting spectacles last" (White, 1959, p. 319). In the current literature is evidence that infants enjoy and can detect contingencies in the physical environment as soon as they have motor control over the behaviors required to produce them (about 12 weeks; Watson, 1966, 1971). Research suggests that infants respond to social contingencies even earlier (Ainsworth, 1979; Bowlby, 1969).

Although there is no incontrovertible proof for a universal human need for competence, some of the most compelling evidence is physiological. Work with humans and other animal species has shown that unpredictability and loss of control are not only psychologically distressing, but also have direct effects on endocrine and immune system functioning (Gunnar, 1980, 1986; Seligman, 1975). Research on the neurophysiological mechanisms responsible for detecting contingencies and regulating links to emotion systems is accumulating (Gunnar, 1986). Connections to the brain, to physiology, and to genetic substrate would be additional evidence that the need for competence is inborn.

*Competence Is Not Autonomy.* The need for self-determination is often confused with competence. The need for self-determination, or autonomy, is the desire to be the origin of one's own behavior, to be free, to choose one's course of action for oneself (DeCharms, 1968; Deci, 1975; Deci & Ryan, 1985). Although both are sources of motivation, they are conceptually and empirically distinct (DeCharms, 1981). Competence refers to the connection between behaviors and outcomes; it is the extent to which a person feels capable of producing desired and preventing undesired events; [its] opposite . . . is helplessness. Autonomy refers to the connection between volition and action; it is the extent to which a person feels free to show the behaviors of his choice; nonautonomous behaviors include both compliance and defiance, which have in common that they are reactions to others' agendas and not freely chosen. (Patrick, Skinner, & Connell, 1993, p. 782)

## When Needs Are Acquired Versus Innate

The position that the need for competence is innate and universal can be contrasted with social learning approaches, which assume that perceived control is the cognitive residue of reinforcement history, and with acquired needs theories, which assume that needs are socialized. Any theory based on the assumption that the source of motivation is originally external, differs fundamentally from theories based on universal human needs.

According to theories that assume that needs are the product of socialization, social forces convince some people to desire certain things, such as achievement. The individual differences of interest are in the level of acquired need, and their origins are in child-rearing or other external factors. Because level of needs is based on socialization history, the relationship between history, amount of need, and behavior is linear. The more socialization a person has received, the higher the level of need, and the more corresponding behavior will be seen. A person can be "oversocialized," in that they need too much achievement, or are obsessed with control. People who feel little need for achievement or control are seen as overlooked, as not (yet) socialized toward that need. Differences between groups on their behaviors are seen as resulting from differences in socialization values and practices.

This view, in which the source of needs is external, is fundamentally different from a view of psychological needs as intrinsic. Because the notion of innate psychological needs is foreign to most psychologists, the implications of this position will be illustrated using a metaphor based on well-understood needs, those based in physiology.

Control experiences are to the need for competence as water is to thirst. Thirst is not socialized, and if one wanted to examine the behaviors motivated by thirst, one would not start with the examination of individual differences in the need for water, nor would one look at the extent to which society convinces people to be thirsty. One would examine the extent to which people had been allowed access to water. The difference between people who are desperately seeking water and ones who are satisfied is not how much they require water, in any real sense, but how recently and fully they have had something to drink. In a similar vein, people who have given up on the quest for water are not considered to be undersocialized, instead, they are considered to be on the brink of dying from thirst.

Parallel implications can be drawn for theories in which the need for competence is assumed to be innate. If individual differences in need are the target, then the sources studied are not socialization history, but genetics, physiology, and temperament. Following birth, individual differences in the level of need are not very informative; differences in the extent to which interactions with the context allow people to fulfill this need are. How does a passive helpless person differ from someone who pursues competence experiences in a zestful, interested way? Does the depressed individual require less competence than the active one? According to an innate needs theory, the difference between these people is not in their need for competence, but in their histories of control experiences, and on the extent to which they believe they can meet the need.

## Arguments Against the Need for Competence

Although needs theories of personality and motivation flourished 30 years ago (Cofer, 1985; Deci, 1992; Murray, 1938), today it is undeniably controversial to posit an innate universal need (Rodin, Rennert, & Solomon, 1980). In addition to the general position that nothing is innate or universal, three more specific objections can be raised.

*Individual Differences.* If the need for competence is universal, then why are such big differences between people observed in its expression? The answer lies in genetic and physiological variation. Just as with biological needs like hunger, thirst, and sex, people should be born varying widely in the intensity of their psychological needs. This would result in inborn differences in sensitivity to and detection of contingencies, interest in creating effects, focus of attention, and intensity of emotional responsiveness to contingent stimulation. Collectively referred to as *mastery motivation* (Morgan & Harmon, 1984), such differences have been documented in the first six months of life.

*Developmental Differences.* If the need for competence is present from birth to death, why are there such marked age differences in its expression? Isn't it obvious that young children have much more of it than older children or adults? Decreases in the strength of competence strivings with age can, of course, be considered evidence for the innate nature of the need. The shorter the time the social context has to undermine the need, the less diminished will be its expression. Alternatively, instead of arguing that the strength of the need decreases with age, one could argue that the contextual constraints on the experience and expression of competence increase with age.

Young children express their competence needs in rich and relatively unconstrained contexts, such as family homes, playgrounds, yards, and parks. Older children and adults are supposed to have their needs for competence met in the worlds of school and work, although it is clear that these institutions do not accomplish this. The steady deterioration of children's motivation for schooling from preschool to high school can be seen as an indicator of this problem (Harter, 1983). Such constraints affect its *expression*, but they cannot extinguish the basic need for competence itself. For example, educators have been relieved to discover that they can still tap into reservoirs of interest and enthusiasm, when the activities required by schools are brought into line with individuals' interests (Ames & Ames, 1984, 1985). When children are allowed to design model airplanes or build theaters, interventions produce sudden shifts from passivity, apathy, and absenteeism, to involvement, participation, and excitement, even for the most "unreachable" children. Likewise, when adults are seen in rich and unconstrained contexts, the expression of their need for competence reappears. Passionate, enthusiastic involvement is the hallmark of hobbies and volunteer work, and of artists, scientists, and entrepreneurs.

*Cultural Differences.* Finally, if the need for competence is universal, why does it not appear in all cultures? Isn't this fixation on competence a uniquely Western proclivity? This question, just like the issue of whether this need has been present across all historical time, is basically unanswerable. We don't know much about all the diverse populations within Western cultures, much less the rest of the world. We do know that the interest in competence and the stressfulness of uncontrollability are found in other species, such as monkeys, dogs, and rats (Seligman, 1975; Weinberg & Levine, 1980). This suggests that the need might be present in all members of our species as well.

There is currently no compelling evidence that this need is only a Western phenomenon, even though the contexts, constraints, and channels for its expression surely differ across cultures (Little, Oettingen, Stetsenko, & Baltes, 1994a; Oettingen, 1994; Oettingen, Little, Lindenberger, & Baltes, 1994; Stetsenko, Little, Oettingen, & Baltes, in press). Counterarguments that members of some cultures do not have a need for competence often confuse this need with other needs, such as power or achievement. Further, the need for competence is often equated with the value system of individualism, and then contrasted with a collective or group mentality (Markus & Kitayama, 1991; Meyer, 1990; Schooler, 1990). These value systems refer, on the one hand, to the goals set by a society (individual vs. group advancement) and, on the other, to the means for reaching them (individual vs. group action). The need for competence is orthogonal to both specific means and ends. An individual will feel competent to the extent he or she can (a) individually produce individual outcomes, *or* (b) as a part of a group, contribute to collective outcomes, or both. Societies affect whether their members succeed or fail to meet the need for competence, not depending on the means and goals societies value, but depending on the contingencies provided between them. An individualistic society interferes with people be paid for violating this need, in disaffection, depression, and apathy. It is ultimately an optimistic meta-theory, because it holds that motivation is intrinsic. If social contexts can manage to set up opportunities, people will actively strive to become more competent.

meeting their needs if it does not allow individuals to
through their own efforts, and a collective society underm
ples' needs if it sets up a system in which groups are no
produce desired results through their collective action.

## Implications of a Needs Theory

The assumption of innate universal needs makes some
nervous. Many people feel more comfortable in explaining
for competence as a human right, arguing that all childrer
right to feel and be competent. If postulating a universal in
for competence is so controversial, then why do it? Beca
explanatory power and because it organizes theories arou
active agentic individual. A need for competence explains
of control and the universal psychological devastation of
explains why everyone constructs maps in their heads a
to produce desired and avoid undesired effects. It exp
beliefs about control are not just cold cognitions, like c
facts, but instead are hot convictions filled with emotion an
meaning and capable of propelling people into action o
them in their tracks.

Theories in which people intrinsically desire to interact
with their social and physical environments look very diff
theories in which humans have no basic needs. Postulat
for competence gives ultimate power to individuals as s
agents of their own motivation. It specifies that all peop
internal prerequisites for the development of well-functi
petence systems. It makes strong prescriptions about op
texts; they should be organized to provide individuals v
tunities to meet these universal needs. It imposes limitat
power of contexts as well. Social agents cannot determi
or not people will desire to be competent; that is decid
human nature. Social agents can only decide whether pe
given opportunities to experience themselves as compe
ever, if humans have a need for competence, then a price

# PART II

# Constructs of Control

# Are All Perceived Control Constructs the Same?

When approaching the area, it is easy to be daunted by the thicket of constructs clustered around the general notion of a sense of control. Are they all similar, are they simply "control by any other name" (Rodin, 1990)? Or, are they completely different, examining separate facets of the experience of control? Careful reading suggests that they are somehow distinctive but also somehow interrelated, maybe even overlapping. How can one begin to think about these constructs, let alone make a decision about their usefulness, until their relative roles in the process of control are clarified?

The notion that humans have an inborn need for competence has interesting implications for sorting out different theories of perceived control. It establishes common ground among all conceptions, and also provides a framework for analyzing their differences. From this perspective, the need for competence launches the striving for effective interactions with the social and physical environments. As White (1959) states, "Effectance motivation . . . aims for the feeling of efficacy" (p. 323). These experiences then become part of the individual's self-system processes, in the form of a sense of control, which in turn guides future actions.

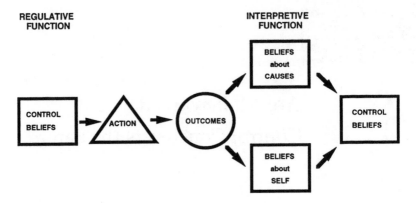

**Figure 3.1.** A Schematic of the Competence System

Accordingly, all beliefs about control are part of a larger system, referred to here as the *competence system,* which has the function of regulating and interpreting goal-directed interactions with the environment (Connell, 1990; Connell & Wellborn, 1991; Harter, 1978; Skinner, 1991a). Hence, all theories of perceived control are attempts to map the competence system. These theories have in common that they try to explain how control experiences contribute to the construction of beliefs, and how these beliefs in turn promote or undermine effective interactions. The theories differ in the specific part of that process on which they focus.

A simple overview of the competence system (see Figure 3.1) depicts a sequence in which individuals' beliefs contribute to their action, which then influences the success of their actual performances, which in turn has an impact on their beliefs. As can be seen, beliefs have two functions in an action sequence: (a) before and during engagement, they regulate the quality of action, and (b) after engagement, they interpret the performance. The focus of each of the major theories of perceived control can be located relative to this action sequence.

## Four Major Theories of Perceived Control

At least four major theories can be identified, organized around the constructs locus of control, causal attributions, learned helplessness, and self-efficacy. In order to provide main reference points in the comparison of these theories, an outline of the central ideas in each is provided. The analysis of the place of each construct in the competence system more generally should be helpful in specifying their overlap as well as identifying dimensions upon which they differ fundamentally.

*Locus of Control.* Embedded in a social learning framework, locus of control was originally the expectancy term in a mathematically explicit expectancy-value model (Crandall & Battle, 1970; Lefcourt, 1982; Rotter, 1966). The locus of control construct, divorced from the value term, was soon considered almost exclusively as an individual difference variable (Rotter, 1990). In its original formulation, it was defined as follows:

> When a reinforcement is perceived by the subject as following some action of his own but not being entirely contingent upon his action, then in our culture, it is typically perceived as the result of luck, chance, fate, as under the control of powerful others, or as unpredictable because of the great complexity of forces surrounding him. When the event is interpreted in this way by an individual, we have labeled this a belief in external control. If the person perceives that the event is contingent upon his own behavior or relatively permanent characteristics, we have termed this a belief in internal control. (Rotter, 1966, p. 1)

Hence, the key construct consists of a single bipolar internal-external dimension, with an internal locus of control predicting a variety of positive outcomes in the domains of achievement, health, sports, work, marriage, and psychological adjustment (Lefcourt, 1981, 1983, 1992; Strickland, 1989). Many other theories of motivation also contain an action-outcome expectancy as a summary term (e.g., probability of success, outcome expectation; Atkinson, 1957; Dweck & Elliott, 1983; Heckhausen, 1977; Vroom, 1964).

*Causal Attributions.* Taking issue with a specific finding in the locus of control literature, namely, the link between internality and expectancy shifts, Weiner argued that the causes used to distinguish the internal-external dimension (skill vs. chance) also differed on another key dimension: stability. By contrasting causes that differed along both these dimensions, he demonstrated that the stability of the causes to which outcomes are attributed actually is the key to predicting expectancy shifts (with unstable, and not external, causes producing shifts; Weiner, Nierenberg, & Goldstein, 1976).

Building on this work, Weiner developed a theory of causal attributions (Weiner, 1985a). Weiner posited that when something negative or unexpected happens, people ask themselves why. The causes to which they attribute events can be arrayed along a number of dimensions, the most important of which are internality, stability, controllability, and intentionality. These dimensions predict many important outcomes, such as emotions, behaviors, and motivation. This theory has spawned literally hundreds of studies of the causes and effects of attributions, ranging from achievement and work outcomes to recovery from rape, life-threatening illness, and traumatic accidents.

*Learned Helplessness.* The classical work examined the links between exposure to noncontingency and subsequent cognitive, behavioral, and motivational deficits (Seligman, 1975). The key proposition was that when people and other animals (e.g., dogs and rats) experience aversive events that occur independently of their own responses, they do not just learn that specific behaviors are ineffective. They learn that no effective responses exist, that they are helpless. As a result, when they are subsequently placed in situations in which events actually are objectively contingent, these perceptions are generalized, and people behave as if they were still in a noncontingent situation. The three major effects studied in classical learned helplessness experiments were (a) behavioral deficits, or lack of response initiation and passivity; (b) cognitive deficits, or impaired detection of actual contingencies; and (c) emotional deficits, or depression.

About a decade after it was introduced, Seligman and his colleagues published a cognitive reformulation designed to specify one set of mechanisms by which noncontingency produces its syndrome of deficits (Abramson, Seligman, & Teasdale, 1978). Recalling other theories of causal attribution, the reformulation posited that following experiences of noncontingency, individuals make explanations about its causes that can be arrayed along the dimensions of internality, stability, and globality. The stability of the cause predicts the chronicity of the deficits; globality influences their generality; and internality determines the extent to which self-esteem will be affected. Research on both the classical and reformulated models of helplessness continue, especially in the areas of achievement, health, sports, and depression.

*Self-Efficacy.* The year before the learned helplessness reformulation was published, a persuasive summary of research appeared supporting a new expectancy construct: self-efficacy (Bandura, 1977). In his formulation, Bandura noted that most theories of perceived control concentrated on beliefs about the effectiveness of responses in producing outcomes (which he referred to as response-outcome expectancies). However, these expectancies should have no effect on behavior unless one also has "the conviction that one can successfully execute the behavior required to produce the outcome" (Bandura, 1977, p. 193). These latter beliefs, referred to as *efficacy expectations,* were the basis for a new area of research, examining the effects of self-efficacy on behavior, emotion, and motivation. Work in this area was concentrated initially on failures of behavioral regulation, such as in phobias or noncompliance with medical regimes. However, its influence has also spread widely, to research in education, social relationships, sports, and the workplace.

## Constructs in the Competence System

The attempt to analyze theories of locus of control, causal attributions, learned helplessness, and self-efficacy begins with the assumption that each is part of the competence system. Figure 3.2 depicts the competence system with each construct located within it. This analysis indicates that these constructs differ (a) on the extent to which they function primarily to regulate or interpret performance, and (b) on whether they influence behavior and emotion directly or indirectly.

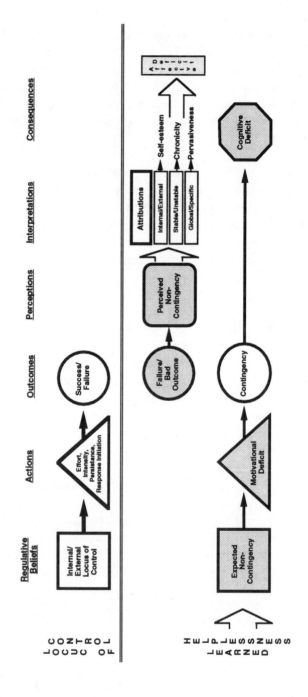

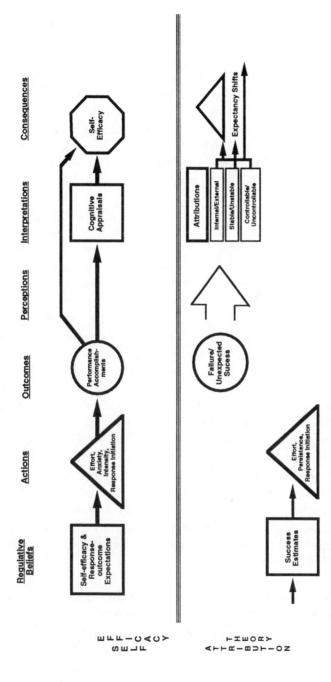

**Figure 3.2.** A Schematic of How Each of the Major Theories of Perceived Control Fits Into the Competence System

25

*Interpretation Versus Regulation.* One of the biggest differences among the four major theories is whether they focus on beliefs that regulate action versus those that interpret performances. Self-efficacy theory focuses directly on the expectations that regulate action. Of secondary interest are performance interpretations that shape subsequent levels of efficacy expectations. In contrast, causal attribution theories focus on beliefs that are interpretations of performances. These interpretations or attributions can contribute to current emotions and motivation; they also have an impact on subsequent expectations for control.

*Proximal Versus Distal.* As can be seen from Figure 3.2, beliefs that regulate behavior are closer in the causal chain to implementation of action than are beliefs that interpret performance. Regulatory beliefs, such as self-efficacy and performance expectations, are hypothesized to directly precede behavior in the causal chain; hence, in situations in which they are used, they will have strong relations to behavior. In contrast, beliefs that interpret performance, such as causal attributions, are more distal predictors of action. They are by definition used in the episode preceding the target action, and thus many events can intervene between an attribution and a subsequent performance. As can also be seen in Figure 3.2, the effects of performance attributions on action will be mediated by performance expectancies (regulatory beliefs).

Hence, in general, regulatory beliefs will have a bigger effect on action than will interpretative beliefs. Interpretative beliefs will have their most proximal effect on emotions. Expectations of control should have a generalized effect on joy and fear (or anxiety), but the differentiated emotions, such as pride, shame, anger, and pity, rely on the interpretation of performance. Hence, predictions of emotional reactions to performance outcomes should be best predicted by attributional theories.

*General Versus Specific.* There are other dimensions upon which these four theories differ. Some are not integral to the conceptualizations themselves but are integral to the empirical success of the constructs. The most notable of these is the generality versus specificity of beliefs (Berry & West, 1993). This refers to how narrowly the perception of control is indexed to a specific domain, situation, behavior, or event. At one end of the continuum are very general beliefs, which apply across a broad range of experiences and areas of life, for example, "If I want something enough, I can get it." At the other end are beliefs tied to single events, such as, "I can lift a weight of 15 pounds."

The specific-general distinction is orthogonal to the four conceptualizations described. A person can have generalized locus of control or generalized efficacy or a general explanatory style. However, each of the four theories is identified with a measurement model that can be placed along this continuum. At the most general pole are the explanatory styles of learned helplessness. These measures tap beliefs across a range of domains and average them as an index of a general style of interpreting positive and negative events (Abramson et al., 1978). Originally, locus of control assessments were even more general; instead of being averaged across domains, they did not include domain referents at all. However, current measures of locus of control are for the most part domain specific (Crandall, Katkovsky, & Crandall, 1965; Lachman, 1986a; Lefcourt, 1981; Wallston, 1992). Causal attributions are typically assessed in actual or hypothetical situations, and so are even more specific than locus of control measures. Most specific of all have tended to be efficacy expectations. These are usually assessed as judgments about individual behaviors or levels of a task (e.g., subtraction problems of increasing difficulty).

What is the importance of recognizing that theories are independent from the level of specification of their assessments? Independent of the particular theory, it is clear that specificity of assessment has a major impact on the magnitude of relationships to target behavior and performance. For example, in a study of cognitive aging, Lachman (1986a) demonstrated that domain-specific locus of control beliefs were related to cognitive performance, whereas generalized beliefs were not. In a study of children, Connell (1985) likewise demonstrated the discriminatory connections between academic, sports, and social perceptions of control and outcomes in the corresponding domains.

The more specific the belief, the larger the relationship to that specific behavior. The limitations of specific beliefs are also clear. The more specific the belief, the fewer behaviors it predicts outside the specific situation. Because it is tempting to value high correlations more than scope of application, it is easy to conclude that constructs with more specific measures, such as self-efficacy, are more powerful than constructs with more general measures, such as explanatory styles. This would be a mistake. The decision about which construct to use should be made independently of the decision about the level of generality of the measurement.

In sum, major theories of control differ on whether they focus on beliefs that regulate or interpret control experiences, on whether they examine the experience of mastery or helplessness (or both success and failure), on how distal constructs are from the consequences of emotion and behavior, and on the measurement models typically used to examine control-related beliefs. Nevertheless, each can be viewed as tapping an interrelated component of the competence system.

# 4

# Who Needs a New Conceptualization of Perceived Control?

If major theories of perceived control focus on different parts of the same process, can they then be considered in conjunction in order to examine the competence system as a whole? Is there anything to be gained from a more comprehensive analysis of the entire profile of control-related beliefs? Some researchers think so. Individual differences researchers suggest that interactions among beliefs may be better predictors of performance than single constructs. For example, locus of control for health may moderate the relation between efficacy and health-promoting behaviors (Wallston, 1992). And, developmental researchers point out that different aspects of control may have differential developmental trajectories. For example, beliefs about an internal locus of control seem to remain stable as people age, whereas beliefs about the role of powerful others and chance increase (Lachman, 1986a).

Although the entire range of control constructs would not be included in every empirical analysis, it might nevertheless be useful, for any given problem, to consider the entire range of beliefs before selecting those that are relevant. The use of multiple control constructs in single studies also makes it possible to investigate the connections among beliefs, analyzing their unique, differential, additive, and synergistic effects. Perhaps some sets of beliefs are more important in predicting certain outcomes or in certain domains and age groups. For example, helplessness may be a better explanation for performance deficits in younger children, whereas perceived ability may play a bigger role for adolescents (Skinner, 1991a).

The conceptualization presented here is based on an attempt to differentiate and integrate major constructs from theories of locus of control, causal attributions, learned helplessness, self-efficacy, and summary performance expectations (Skinner, Chapman, & Baltes, 1988b). It was originally designed as a vehicle for containing other constructs, but in the process of constructing the framework, the conceptualization took on a shape of its own. It no longer maps directly back to other theories, but it may still prove useful in identifying individual beliefs as well as combinations or profiles of perceived control.

## The Conceptualization

The conceptualization was based in an action theoretical perspective. Action theory views actions, instead of behaviors or responses, as central units of analysis (Boesch, 1976; Frese & Sabini, 1985). Actions are defined as goal-directed, intentional, emotion-laden behaviors that take place in a social context. For the current conceptualization, the action-theoretical distinction among agents, means, and ends was central. Naive accounts of action involve not only an understanding of the agent's role in producing outcomes, but also of the connection between means and ends, and between agents and means. This observation led to differentiation among beliefs about the connection between agents and ends; between means and ends; and between agents and means.

Three sets of beliefs can be defined: (a) *control beliefs* refer to generalized expectancies about the extent to which the self can produce desired or prevent undesired events; (b) *strategy (or means-ends) beliefs* refer to generalized expectancies about the extent to which certain

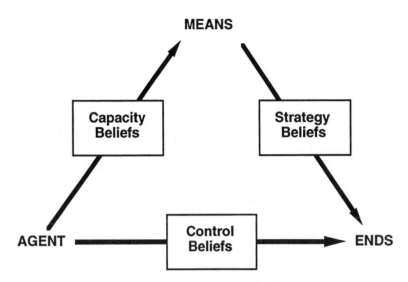

**Figure 4.1.** A Distinction Among Three Kinds of Beliefs
SOURCE: Adapted from Skinner, Chapman, & Baltes, 1988b.

means or causes are sufficient conditions for the production of ends or outcomes; and (c) *capacity (or agency) beliefs* refer to generalized expectancies about the extent to which the self possesses or has access to certain causes (Skinner et al., 1988b). These are pictured graphically in Figure 4.1.

In this framework, the term *beliefs* is used to emphasize the nature of the control perceptions. Beliefs denote convictions rather than more cerebral and reality-based judgments, estimates, or evaluations. Beliefs denote cognitive constructions and so are open to revision. Beliefs can refer to the future (e.g., capacity expectations) or the past (e.g., strategy attributions). They can also be used at any level of generality from the most situation specific to the most global.

These three belief sets are hypothesized to function in the regulation and interpretation of action. The primary regulatory beliefs are beliefs about control, but strategy and capacity beliefs can also be used to regulate action more specifically, for example, in forming an action plan (Chapman & Skinner, 1985; Skinner, in press). However, strategy and capacity beliefs have their primary function in interpreting performance. They are both used to understand the meaning of successes and failures and are themselves influenced by patterns of action and performance outcomes.

The functional relationships among the belief sets is an open empirical question. Conceptually, they are considered to be distinct. Semantically, of course, control beliefs are equivalent to a combination of strategy and capacity beliefs. If one has the capacity to execute an effective strategy then one has control. However, there is no basis for assuming that functional relations mirror semantic relations or that belief systems are logical or rational. Aside from the fact that these relations probably differ at different ages (Weisz, 1986), it is also possible that the beliefs may be formed based on different kinds of experiences, that they may have different functions, or that they may be formed at different levels of generality. Hence, we decided to assume that each set of beliefs represents a separate cognitive construction, and to use empirical information to analyze the tenability of this assumption in different domains and age groups.

*The Distinction.* The distinction between beliefs about the causes of outcomes and about the access of the causes to the self is present in many theories of control. The distinction was critical in early sociological thinking about political action (see Gurin & Brim, 1984, for a review), in which "system responsiveness" defined as "judgments of the environment's likely response to an individual's action" is contrasted with "personal efficacy" or "judgments of the self as able to produce acts that should lead to desirable outcomes" (Gurin & Brim, 1984, p. 285). In psychology, it is most prominent in the distinction between response-outcome expectations and efficacy expectations (Bandura, 1977). It is contained in expectancy-value theories as the difference between action-outcome expectancies and outcome-consequence expectancies (Heckhausen, 1977) or between instrumentality and expectancy (Vroom, 1964).

The distinction is also depicted in the reformulation of learned helplessness theory as the difference between universal and personal helplessness, described as "cases in which the individual as well as other individuals do not possess controlling responses" versus "cases in which an individual lacks requisite controlling responses that are available to other people" (Abramson et al., 1978, p. 51). The distinction also figures prominently in the developmental theory of Weisz and colleagues (Weisz, 1983; Weisz & Stipek, 1982). They contrast judgments of contingency or "the degree to which outcomes in the situation are contingent on people's behavior," with those of competence or "one's own competence to produce the necessary behavior" (Weisz, 1983, p. 234).

In comparing our conceptualization with other theories that incorporate this distinction, several major differences are apparent. First, although all theories include beliefs that are analogous to strategy and capacity beliefs, not all theories include beliefs analogous to control beliefs. The seriousness of this omission remains to be seen. Control beliefs are analogous to performance expectations and success estimates, which have turned out to be key predictors of action in value-expectancy models of motivation. If control beliefs are, as we hypothesize, the aspect of perceived control that regulates action, then it might be important to include them in any profile of control-related beliefs. If, on the other hand, control beliefs are reducible to a combination of strategy and capacity beliefs, then their absence will not be problematic. Of course, unless control beliefs are included in assessments, we cannot answer these questions empirically.

A second difference between ours and similar conceptualizations is that our theory incorporates constructs not only from those theories that are based on the strategy-capacity distinction, but also from those that are not, such as locus of control, attribution, and reformulated learned helplessness. Other theories that include the distinction between beliefs about causes and beliefs about the self consider only one category of causes, responses. That is, all beliefs analogous to strategy beliefs refer to the effectiveness of *behavior* or *responses* in producing outcomes, and all beliefs analogous to capacity beliefs refer to beliefs about the access to the self of *responses*. In contrast, our conceptualization explicitly refers to a broad range of causal categories. For example, in the academic domain, we have considered both strategy and capacity beliefs for the causal categories effort, ability, powerful others, and luck. Research from locus of control and attribution theories documents that beliefs about uncontrollable and external causes are an important component of profiles of perceived control.

*Independence of Belief Sets.* The third difference between our theory and ones based on an analogous distinction is that we have emphasized the importance of defining and operationalizing strategy and capacity beliefs independently. It is not surprising that attribution theories, which are not based on the distinction between beliefs about the self versus about causes, combine strategy *and* capacity beliefs in causal attributions. An attribution of *success* to a cause ("I did well because I tried hard") implies both that the cause is effective in producing the outcome ("effort is important to success") *and* that the self has access to that cause ("I can try hard"). In contrast, an attribution of *failure* to a cause ("I failed because of ability") implies both that the cause is effective in producing the outcome ("ability is important to success") *and* that the self does not have access to that cause ("I'm dumb"). This has an impact on the interpretation of the "active ingredient" in causal attributions. For example, when contrasting attributions for effort versus ability, they differ not only on the nature of the causes, as is pointed out by attribution theories, but also on beliefs about the self (i.e., "I didn't try hard" vs. "I'm stupid").

Even when it is an explicit goal of a theory to separate beliefs about causes from beliefs about the self, it is easy to confound them. In fact, in reviewing the definitions of beliefs analogous to capacity beliefs, it is clear that most theories described have done so (cf. Heckhausen, 1977). For example, if self-efficacy judgments are defined as "the conviction that one can successfully execute the behavior required to produce the outcome" (Bandura, 1977, p. 193) then a self-efficacy judgment presupposes the existence of an effective response, that is, it implies a positive response-outcome expectancy. As currently defined, most beliefs about agent-means relations (i.e., efficacy expectations, personal efficacy, and competence judgments) imply beliefs about means-ends relations as well.

Two consequences of this situation can be noted. First, when these constructs are used, any conclusions drawn about agent-means beliefs are really conclusions about both belief sets. For example, any conclusions about the beneficial effects of high self-efficacy should be interpreted as effects of high self-efficacy combined with high response-outcome expectations. Second, any interventions that are based on research showing the salutary effects of beliefs analogous to self-efficacy should recall that the replication of these effects will require changing not only self-efficacy expectations, but also response-outcome expectations as well.

## Beliefs Specific to Domain and Developmental Level

In realizing the current conceptualization, we emphasized the distinction among the three belief sets, as well as considered the causal categories, valence, domains, and specificity of beliefs, and the developmental level of the respondents. The priority of maintaining the belief sets as operationally distinct involved designing a general format for each kind of item (see Table 4.1). As can be seen, strategy and capacity beliefs are independent. A person can be high on capacity ("I have all the means") and still report low strategy beliefs ("But none of the means produce any outcomes"). Or a person can be high on strategy beliefs ("There are lots of means that lead to

**TABLE 4.1** The General Format for Generating Items Tapping Control, Strategy, and Capacity Beliefs

| Belief Type | Positive | Negative |
| --- | --- | --- |
| Control Beliefs | If I want to, I can produce a success outcome. ("If I want to, I can do well in school.") | No matter how hard I try, I cannot avoid a failure outcome. ("No matter how I try, I can't keep from fighting with my friends."). |
| Strategy Beliefs | If I want to get success, this cause must be present. ("If I want to do well in school, I have to be smart.") | If this cause is not present, I will fail. ("If I don't hang out with the popular kids, I won't have any friends.") |
| Capacity Beliefs | I have this cause. ("I can try hard in school.") | I don't have the cause. ("I don't have the brains to do well in school"). |

outcomes") but still perceive him- or herself as lacking in capacity ("But I don't have any of them").[1]

*Domain and Generality.* The domain-specific instantiation of these beliefs requires a decision about the means and the ends. The "ends" are the success and failure outcomes of interest, basically the specific desired and undesired events. Along with most researchers in this area, we decided to strike a balance between scope and precision, such that we would maximize the relationship between beliefs and outcomes by using domain-specific beliefs, but we would also maximize the range of outcomes to which beliefs would relate by using fairly general outcomes within each domain. Specifically, we operationalized beliefs in the domains school and friendship, and used as outcomes fairly general events in those domains. For example, in the school domain, we used outcomes such as "do well in school" and "get good grades."

*Causal Categories.* Although one difference between our theory and others that rely on the strategy-capacity distinction is that we incorporate multiple causal categories in our conceptualization, our theory does not specify a priori just what those categories of means should be. In fact, we expect that they would vary based on the domain of the outcome and the developmental level of the respondents. For example, young children do not usually refer to outcomes as based on chance (Connell, 1985), which is an important category for the elderly (Lachman, 1986b). Children also do not think in terms of macro-environmental factors, such as political and economic climate, as influencing important outcomes, although is an important factor in adult thinking (Brandtstaedter, 1989; Gurin & Brim, 1984; J. Heckhausen, 1991).

Our choice of causal categories has relied on research carried out by attribution and learned helplessness theorists on the important *dimensions* of causes. So, for example, we have always tried to include in our categories causes that seem open to voluntary control (e.g., behavior), causes that are uncontrollable (e.g., attributes), causes that are external (e.g., powerful others), and unknown causes. Unknown causes, a new category for most researchers, refer to beliefs that one simply doesn't know the causes of success and failure in a particular domain (Connell, 1985).

Our measurement development work has also been informed by open-ended interviews about the causes of outcomes in the domains of interest with respondents of our target age group. In other words, using the template of causal dimensions provided by theorists, we have found it most useful to listen to respondents about the actual causal categories included. In well-understood domains, such as health, this may not be needed; or in domains that are closely parallel to academics, such as sports, a more direct correspondence between categories may be the rule. However, an exploration of naive causal understanding may be essential in creating meaningful causal categories for tapping beliefs in new domains, such as friendships or family relations, or in understudied populations, such as the elderly or minorities.

## Profiles of Perceived Control

A measure of perceived control in the academic domain (see items in Figure 4.2 and the Appendix) allowed for an empirical test of the distinction among control, strategy, and capacity beliefs (Skinner et al., 1988b). At both the item and scale level, the three belief sets, although related, are factorially distinct. The invariance of the measurement model has been replicated across diverse samples (Little, Oettingen, Stetsenko, & Baltes, 1994b). The three belief sets also differentially relate, as predicted, to other control scales. For example, strategy but not capacity beliefs scales are closely related to measures of locus of control. They manifest differential developmental trajectories across middle childhood; for example, capacity beliefs remain fairly stable whereas strategy beliefs for causes like powerful others, luck, and unknown decline rapidly (Skinner & Chapman, 1987; Skinner, Chapman, & Baltes, 1988a). Each may have differential antecedent experiences (Skinner, 1991a).

The three belief sets also show differential and unique relations to outcomes (Chapman, Skinner, & Baltes, 1990; Little et al., 1994a; Oettingen et al., 1994; Skinner et al., 1988a; Weigel, Wertlieb, &

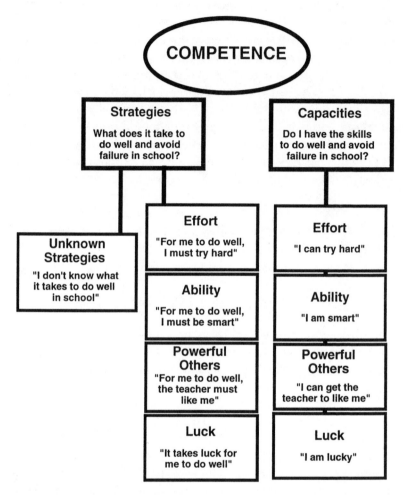

**Figure 4.2.** A Measure of Children's Control, Strategy, and Capacity Beliefs in the Academic Domain
SOURCE: Wellborn, Connell, & Skinner, 1988.

Feldstein, 1989; Weisz, 1986). For example, in the academic domain, an examination of the different beliefs that predict children's engagement versus disaffection in school during middle childhood (Skinner, Wellborn, & Connell, 1990) revealed that children's engagement was promoted by (positively correlated with) control beliefs as well as capacity beliefs for effort and ability; engagement was undermined by beliefs in the effectiveness of nonaction means, including strategy beliefs for powerful others, luck, and unknown factors. Highest levels of engagement were found for children who reported that effort was an effective means and that they had the capacity to exert effort (high strategy and capacity for effort). Lowest levels of engagement were found for children who reported that nonaction means were critical to success but that they themselves did not have the capacity to enact those means (high strategy and low capacity for ability, powerful others, and luck).

*Profiles of Perceived Control.* The new conceptualization allows the construction of a more comprehensive and differentiated picture of the range of perceived control that might characterize an individual's thinking in a particular domain at a particular age. For example, strategy by capacity interactions suggest that "interaction scores" may be useful in characterizing children's beliefs in causal categories; the belief that ability is essential for success and that I lack it (high strategy and low capacity beliefs) is more debilitating than either belief alone or even than their additive effect.

Beliefs can also be combined to construct "profiles" of control (see Figure 4.3). Optimal beliefs include: high control beliefs ("I can produce success and prevent failure"), high strategy and capacity for effort ("effort is an effective cause and I can try hard"), low ability strategy and high capacity ("ability is not that critical but I am smart"), low strategy and high capacity for powerful others ("teachers are not running the show but I can get them to like me"), low strategy and high capacity for luck ("luck is not essential to success but I am lucky"), and low unknown strategy beliefs ("I know the causes for success and failure").

A variety of nonoptimal profiles of perceived control can also be constructed (see Figure 4.3). In fact, simply missing any of the elements of the optimal profile can be considered maladaptive in itself. Cumulatively, the most maladaptive profile would include: low control beliefs ("I cannot produce success or prevent failure"), high strategy and low capacity for effort ("effort is an effective cause but

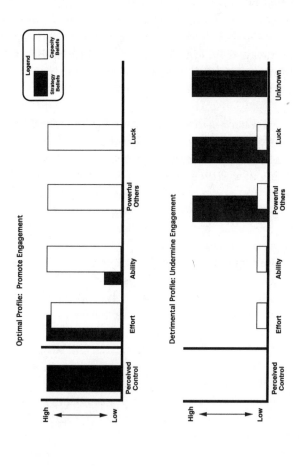

**Figure 4.3.** Profiles of Perceived Control Predicted to Promote and Undermine Engagement

I cannot try hard"), high ability strategy and low capacity ("ability is critical but I am dumb"), high powerful others strategy and low capacity ("teachers are running the show but I can't get them to like me"), high strategy and low capacity for luck ("luck is essential to success but I am unlucky"), and high unknown strategy beliefs ("I have no idea what causes success and failure").

In sum, a new conceptualization of perceived control has been suggested, based on the distinction among agents, means, and ends, that integrates key constructs from locus of control, learned helplessness, attribution theory, and self-efficacy. Beliefs about the effectiveness of causes (strategy beliefs) are distinguished, conceptually and operationally, from beliefs about the access of causes to the self (capacity beliefs). When these two kinds of beliefs are assessed for a set of domain- and developmentally-relevant causal categories (e.g., effort, powerful others), their effects can be examined individually or as part of a profile of perceived control.

## Note

1. An alternative format used to operationalize strategy beliefs is to inquire about the effectiveness of causes for agents in general (J. Heckhausen, 1991; Little et al., 1994b; Skinner, Chapman, Baltes, 1983), using the general format "When people get an outcome, is it because of this cause?". This also allows for independent assessment of beliefs; one can believe that a certain cause produces an outcome in general (strategy or means-ends beliefs) but that one oneself does not have that cause (capacity or agency beliefs).

# PART III

# Antecedents
of Perceived Control

# 5

# What Are the Origins
# of Perceived Control?

Children construct their beliefs about control cumulatively, through interactions with the environment in which interesting and important outcomes are at stake. When does this process start, and how does it work? The metatheoretical assumption of an innate need suggests that it starts at birth. As described by Gurin and Brim (1984):

> Through interacting with the world the infant early on begins to grasp understanding of causality and at the same time develops good feelings about the self. Both occur together as the infant has effects on the world. In those moments when the infant tries to make interesting experiences continue, one of life's critical dramas takes place. During this drama the infant's earlier nearly exclusive dependence on external causation gives way to a sense of self as causal agent. (pp. 282-283)

A sense of control is grounded in interactions with the environment. What are these "experiences of control"? In answering this question, researchers have typically focused on objective conditions that promote or undermine control, specifically, on contingency between responses and outcomes. However, objective control conditions include *both* the contingencies provided in the social and physical world *and* the competence of the individual to operate them (Weisz, 1983). In addition, objective conditions provide only opportunities for control until the individual *acts* on them, and then perceives and interprets these interactions as indicating control. Hence, an analysis of control experiences involves three different factors: (a) objective control conditions, or actual contingency and competence; (b) individual action, or the initiation and persistence of responses; and (c) subjective control, or how those interactions are perceived and interpreted.

When conceived in this way, it becomes clear that many different social and psychological processes are at work during the production of control experiences. Understanding the origins of control draws from not only learned helplessness research on contingency; but also from attachment research on sensitivity; from mastery motivation studies of individual differences in attention and persistence; and from causal reasoning research, on the cognitive strategies used to detect and evaluate causality and covariation. Hence, an analysis of the origins of control, and especially individual differences in control experiences, considers both the individual and the social and physical context as critical in creating control experiences.

## Perceiving Control

Research shows that, from the first days of life, infants detect and respond with vigor and joy to control experiences. Even neonates detect contingencies between actions and outcomes and respond to them with increased action and anticipatory reactions (Janos & Papousek, 1977; Papousek, 1967; Papousek & Papousek, 1979, 1980). The notion that human organisms are sensitive to contingencies and are equipped to react adaptively to them, referred to as "contingency awareness" (Watson, 1966), is documented by both observational and experimental work. The experimental paradigm, described in Watson (1971), used an ingenious apparatus, in which the turning of a mobile was wired to a pressure-sensitive pillow placed under an infant's head or feet. The apparatus could be used to compare the effects of contingent stimulation, noncontingent stimulation (in which the mobile turned independently of the baby's actions), and no stimulation (stationary mobile). As early as 8 weeks of age, children detected and responded to contingency. Relative to both control groups, infants with the contingent mobiles were more behaviorally active and persistent. Infants also enjoyed their contingent experiences; they laughed, cooed, and generally sent signals of joy to the contingently turning mobiles. Both behavioral and emotional responses were conspicuously absent from infants whose experiences were noncontingent, even though they received as much stimulation from their independently turning mobiles.

This paradigm and its findings spurred a body of research about noncontingency in infancy, examining the descriptive parameters of the phenomenon, such as infants' attention span for contingent events (Millar & Watson, 1979), and the consequences of noncontingent stimulation in the laboratory (Finkelstein & Ramey, 1977) and at home (Watson, 1979). Taken together, the findings show that, from very early ages, infants detect contingencies and respond to them very differently than noncontingent events, and that this experience is generalized and transferred, influencing reactions to contingencies in other situations. Despite the fact that infants cannot yet reflect upon their own competence or environmental contingencies, it seems clear that they can nevertheless experience themselves as agents, as the originators of effective actions and as the causes of outcomes.

## Opportunities for Control

*Contingency.* A landmark in the understanding of control experience was the definition and study of the concept of contingency versus noncontingency (Seligman, 1975). *Contingency* refers to the connection between action and outcomes. When an event quickly, consistently, and discriminatively follows an action, the event is contingent on the action. When an event is just as likely to occur without the action as when the action is present, then the event is independent of, or noncontingently related to, the action (Seligman, 1975). The beauty of this definition is that it separates the issue of contingency from the issues of outcome valence and outcome probability.

Positive as well as negative outcomes can be noncontingent. And an outcome can be very likely to occur and still be independent of action. Sunrise and sunset are often cited as examples in which the outcome probability is 1.0 and yet the contingency is 0.

Contingency between actions and outcomes is a key feature of control experience. As Seligman argues, "I am convinced that certain arrangements of environmental contingencies will produce a child who believes he is helpless—that he cannot succeed—and that other contingencies will produce a child who believes that his responses matter—that he can control his little world" (p. 137).

*Maternal Contingency.* Research on the effects of noncontingency in the laboratory was consistent with research about the role of contingency in parent-child interactions, in which the effects of maternal contingent responsiveness on cognitive and social development has been repeatedly demonstrated (see Gunnar, 1980, or Skinner, 1985b, for reviews). These findings were used as the basis for several successful interventions that had as their goal improving children's motivational and cognitive development by increasing the amount of contingency children experience between their actions and desired outcomes (Ramey, Starr, Pallas, Whitten, & Reed, 1975; Riksen-Walraven, 1978).

How does maternal contingent responsiveness have an effect on infants' cognitive and social development? Theorists speculated that some of these effects are the product of perceived control, in a very rudimentary form. For example, Lewis and Goldberg (1969) state, "the mother is important because it is the contingency between the infant's behavior and her responses that enables the infant to learn that his behavior does have consequences" (p. 82). In their review of the literature, Lamb and Easterbrooks (1981) concluded that

> contingent responsiveness of people has a . . . major consequence for infants. From the repeated occurrence of sequences in which the infant's behavior serves as the stimulus eliciting a predictable adult response, the baby learns that its behavior can elicit environmental consequences. . . . What occurs next is the most important development—the infant recognizes that it is effective, that it can elicit responses and thus partially determine its own experience. (p. 2)

Some controversy exists about whether the earliest source of control is found in interactions with physical objects or with people. The argument in favor of physical objects points out their superior contingency. Objects, because they respond to manipulation according to the immutable laws of physics, provide an infinite amount of consistent, contingent, replicable control experiences. The counterargument points out the demands made by physical objects on the infant's competence. Infants are motorically incapable of producing any effects on physical objects until they are several months old. Parents, on the other hand, despite their lower consistency, are capable of responding contingently to infants' bids and signals from the first days of life. Before the child can intentionally produce effects of its own, parents can nevertheless provide thousands of contingent experiences, for example, between crying and being picked up, between fussing and being fed, between clinging and being hugged.

*Sensitivity.* Noncontingent experiences may be sufficient to undermine a developing sense of control, but contingency per se is probably not sufficient to support the experience of control. Contingency refers to the consistency and discriminativeness of the relation between action and outcome; it is mute about the content of the outcome. To take an extreme example, a mother who, in response to her child's requests for help, consistently and discriminately ridicules him is just as contingent as a mother who provides the requested support. However similar the two experiences are in terms of contingency, they are very different in terms of control. A sense of control requires that the onset of *desired* and the offset of *undesired* events be contingent on the child's behavior.

The term *sensitivity*, coined by attachment theorists, has this dual focus: It refers to both to the contingency of responses and to their appropriateness. Ainsworth (1967) states that sensitivity "implies that signals are received and correctly interpreted and that the response is prompt and appropriate" (p. 198). Decades of studies of children ranging in age from infancy to adolescence, utilizing a variety of indicators of sensitivity, and observing parent-child interactions in settings with different degrees of structure, have consistently found parental sensitivity to be a predictor of concurrent attachment, and also subsequent child engagement and competence.

*Contingency Versus Sensitivity.* The differential effects of contingency versus sensitivity on children's perceived control has been documented empirically (Skinner, 1985b, 1986). The interactions of mothers and their 4½-year-old children as they worked together on a problem-solving task were coded for several kinds of sensitivity (e.g., sensitive responsiveness and sensitive initiation); and the extent of actual contingency between mother and child behaviors was calculated for each dyad using sequential probability analyses. Although contingency was related positively to children's active task engagement and independence, it was not correlated with their perceived control (assessed separately using open-ended interviews). Only indicators of sensitivity predicted children's sense of control. In addition to clarifying the differential effects of contingency versus sensitivity, this is one of the few studies to actually document the direct connection between sensitivity and early perceived control.

*Attachment Versus Competence.* From a control theorist's perspective, an attachment interpretation of the connection between caregiver behavior and child outcomes is too simple. Attachment theorists, not surprisingly, argue that the mediator of the effects of sensitivity on motivation and competence is the attachment itself. However, it may be useful to separate the effects of warm, sensitive, appropriate responsiveness on the attachment system from its effects on the competence system. Sensitivity may indeed lead a child to love the caregiver and to feel lovable him- or herself; called up in stressful or challenging social situations, these feelings of love, trust, and worth would be the basis for adaptive future relationships (Baldwin, 1992; Bowlby, 1969; Crittendon, 1990).

These effects can, however, be distinguished from those of sensitivity on the competence system and perceived control. With sensitive parents, the child, in addition to feeling the world is loving (attachment system), also feels the world is responsive and predictable (competence system). In addition to feeling that the self is lovable (attachment system), the child also feels the self is effective (compe-

tence system). In this case, the competence system, and not the attachment system, is responsible for launching engagement with challenging situations and for supporting persistence in difficult tasks.

Besides a few die-hard control theorists and their counterparts in
attachment, who cares whether the effects of sensitivity are chan-
neled through the attachment or the competence system? When all
is well, the difference is academic. Parents who are sensitive will
have children who function well in both areas. However, insensitive
parents can be of at least two kinds. They can be totally insensitive,
that is, inconsistent *and* inappropriate in their reading and responding to children's signals. Or they can be warm, loving, and caring, but
also inconsistent and chaotic. The detrimental effects of this latter
child-rearing style would be played out, not in attachment, but in
perceived control.

In theorizing about the cognitive constructions through which the
distal effects of early attachment relationships are carried out, attachment theorists have proposed the notion of "internal working
models of attachment relationships" (Bowlby, 1969; Crittendon,
1990). These internal working models include expectations about
the predictability and responsiveness of the social world and about
the effectiveness of the self in eliciting desired responses. These
beliefs are, of course, defining features of perceived control.

## The Role of the Individual in
## the Generation of Control Experiences

According to the meta-theory of an innate need, the source of
motivation is the person, their physiology, their human nature. The
role of the social context is to provide the individual with the opportunity to fulfill the need for effective interactions with the environment. The constructs of contingency and sensitivity describe contexts
that provide these opportunities. However, the meta-theory also
suggests a central role for the individual: acting on the context in an
effort to produce control experiences and actively processing experiences with an eye toward detecting and repeating control episodes.

*Competence.* Although there is no general agreement on the definition of competence, in one sense it can be referred to as the capacity of the individual to produce actions that are required to operate contingencies in the social and physical environment. For example, Ainsworth refers to a child as more competent "to the extent that he can, through his own activity, control the effect the environment will have on him" (Ainsworth & Bell, 1974). Sroufe (1979) echoes this theme in interpreting his findings that sensitivity leads to better adaptation, where *adaptation* is defined as "children's active engagement in the environment, fitting and shaping themselves to that environment and effecting changes in the environment to satisfy needs" (p. 835).

Children's competence plays a role in generating control experiences. In kinesthetic contingencies and in interactions with physical objects, the importance of gross and fine motor competence is obvious. Being able to release an object voluntarily is needed to experience a contingency between letting go of a block and seeing it fall. Less obvious, but noted by many authors, is the child's role in creating social contingencies. The signals that infants send their caregivers are critical determinants of whether the caregivers can respond appropriately (Lewis & Goldberg, 1969). Children whose signals are clear, distinctive, and diagnostic will receive more appropriate contingent responding from their caregivers. Hence, one source of individual differences in control experiences are variations in competence. These are likely to be influenced by genetics (DeFries, Plomin, & Fulker, 1994) as well as by previous developmental history.

*Action.* The role of individual action is critical in generating control experiences (Skinner, 1985a). Even when high contingencies and high competence are available, children experience no control until they act. Although, in general, children's needs for competence provide ample impetus to act on the environment, research on mastery motivation in infancy has documented reliable, individual differences in persistence of engagement with objects (Morgan, Harmon, & Maslin-Cole, 1990), some of which can probably be attributed to genetic or temperamental sources. These include, during the first year of life, individual differences in span and focus of attention;

exploration and curiosity, including holding, touching, mouthing, examining, shaking, and manipulating objects; and practicing of effects. During the second year, they include individual differences in focus and persistent attempts to solve challenging tasks, task orientation, engrossment, enthusiasm, and self-initiated mastery attempts. At all ages, individual differences have been noted in task pleasure, both expressions of positive affect during task interaction and after successful effect production.

## The Origins of Individual Differences in Sense of Control

Taken together, findings from diverse areas suggest that infants come into the world with the desire for control, with the competence to interact with the social and physical environment, and with the ability to detect and respond to contingency. Differences in the sense of control begin at birth. Individuals bring different strengths of interest in and responsiveness to contingencies as well as different levels of competence. Their social worlds are differentially responsive and infants are differentially given opportunities to interact with tasks that provide stimulation contingent on the responses in their repertoires. If infants are initially greeted with noncontingency, this early sense of low control may inhibit subsequent action, which further reduces control experiences. In contrast, early success at producing effects, through its influence on generalized expectancies of control, may boost engagement and hence subsequent control experiences.

# 6

# How Do Social
# Contexts Promote
# and Undermine Control?

Although contexts don't "give" children or adults control, they can provide opportunities for people to exercise control. Or, too often, they can discourage or prevent individuals from experiencing control. Ways in which the social context promotes and undermines control have been studied in both experimental and naturalistic settings of child-rearing, teaching, coaching, medicine, marriage, management, coping, retirement, and caring for institutionalized elderly. Studies examine the effects of interpersonal contingencies, such as parental responsiveness, teacher performance feedback, or support from institutional caregivers, as well as task parameters, such as failure feedback, workload, difficulty level, or noncontingency. What does this research reveal about the social contexts of control? Are there certain necessary or sufficient conditions for the experience of control, or for its loss? Are there different sources of control experiences that are more or less potent?

The heterogeneous array of conditions associated with gains and losses in control makes it difficult, at first glance, to discern common threads across the range of domains and developmental phases. Research on children has closely examined the family and school contexts that influence control. Studies have examined the impact of global dimensions, such as parental warmth, criticism, power assertion, and rational argumentation (Baumrind, 1977; Crandall, 1973; Krampen, 1989; Lewis & Goldberg, 1969). These are supplemented by the observation of more fine-grained categories of adult behavior, such as teacher praise for work or parent intrusion in task performance (e.g., Barker & Graham, 1987; Crandall & Crandall, 1983; Dweck, Davidson, Nelson, & Enna, 1978; Pintrich & Blumenfeld, 1985).

Research on how contexts influence control in adulthood has emphasized the power structures and contingencies in the domains of work (Hoff & Hohner, 1986; Remondet & Hansson, 1993), marriage (Brandtstaedter, Krampen, & Heil, 1986), and health (Rodin, 1986). Important sources of influence on control during adulthood may also come from individual nonnormative life events and from shifting macro-environmental conditions, such as economic recession or societal changes (Gurin & Brim, 1984). Parallel to research on the effects of adults on children, studies have explored the antecedents of parents' and teachers' self-efficacy in their own roles (e.g., Altman, 1993). For example, parent efficacy can be challenged by infants who provide prolonged aversive noncontingent experiences.

Research on the elderly has been especially concerned with how the social contexts of aging may undermine personal control (Baltes & Baltes, 1986; Heckhausen & Schulz, in press; Rodin, 1980; Thompson & Spacapan, 1991). Studies examine adjustment to retirement as a potential loss of control experiences, as well as challenges posed to control by actual declines in health, mobility, or cognitive functioning (Lachman, 1986b). A special topic has been the effect of long-term care institutions on experiences of control (Baltes & Reisenzein, 1986; Langer & Rodin, 1976).

## Structure Versus Chaos

The concept of an innate need for competence gathers together seemingly diverse aspects of the social context and posits that they can be considered to belong to a common construct because they share the function of influencing control experiences. The overarching construct that describes how the context organizes interactions that allow individuals to pursue control experience is referred to as *structure versus chaos* (Connell, 1990; Connell & Wellborn, 1991; Deci & Ryan, 1985; Skinner, 1991a; Skinner & Wellborn, 1994).

At its most general, *structure* refers to provision of information about pathways for interactions with the environment that lead to desired outcomes, as well as provision of support for traveling those pathways. Highly structured contexts provide clear expectations for action and sometimes even instructions for enactment; they provide consistent feedback and are contingent and responsive; challenges are geared at a level appropriate to the individual's competence. Not only are contingencies available, but encouragement for action is supplied, along with information about how to operate the contingencies. When effective strategies are not currently in the repertoire, support for developing them is provided. Social agents explain the structure, providing information about social and physical consequences of actions, and rationales for their connection.

*Chaos* is the opposite of structure. Chaotic contexts are noncontingent, confusing, unpredictable, and objectively uncontrollable. Little or no guidance is provided about expected behavior or about how to operate any contingencies that may exist. Social partners are unresponsive and inconsistent. Challenges are either overwhelming or understimulating. Action is discouraged. No particular support is provided for trying out new strategies or developing new competencies.

*What Structure Is Not.* The same social contexts that influence control also contain other experiences and exert influence over other important self-perceptions as well as behavior and emotion. It is important to distinguish other contextual dimensions and their effects from structure and its effects on control (Connell, 1990; Connell & Wellborn, 1991; Deci & Ryan, 1985; Grolnick & Ryan, 1989). In the childhood research, structure is most often confused with involvement (Lefcourt, 1982), whereas in the aging literature, chaos is most often confused with constraint or coercion (e.g., White & Janson,

1986). Involvement denotes the expression of affection. It includes dedicating time, energy, and resources, as well as being warm, open, and emotionally available. It includes paying attention and listening to the individual, as well as expressing interest, affection, caring, pleasure in, and enjoyment of the individual. Its opposite, neglect, can be seen in social partners who are cold and distant, aloof, and physically or emotionally unavailable. It is possible for a context to be highly structured but neglectful (e.g., the workplace) or to be very involved but chaotic (more likely in families).

Coercive contexts constrain, manipulate, and compel people. They can do so through methods that are overtly coercive, such as punishments and threats, or through more subtle means, such as love withdrawal, guilt induction, competition and comparison, or rewards and bribes (Ryan, 1982). The opposite of coercion is not structure, it is autonomy support (Deci & Ryan, 1985), which describes contexts that defer to the interests and desires of the individual, by allowing freedom of expression and behavior through such means as choice, respect, and minimum constraints and rules. Different combinations of structure and autonomy support are also possible: Contexts can be highly contingent and consistent and still be coercive (e.g., schools), or they can support autonomy but in a chaotic way. Whereas structure (vs. chaos) should have its primary impact on control, involvement (vs. neglect) should influence the self-system processes connected to attachment, and autonomy support (vs. coercion) should have its major impact on self-determination (Connell & Wellborn, 1991).

*Mechanisms of Structure Versus Chaos.* How does the provision of structure promote the experience of control? A consideration of the essential elements of control experiences suggests three pathways by which contexts can facilitate or impede control: (a) by influencing *objective control conditions,* that is, actual contingencies and actual competence; (b) by encouraging or discouraging *action;* and (c) by offering *translations* of individuals' interactions with the environment that favor or discount control.

This perspective expands on theories and research about the sources of control experiences to specify the content of what the individual takes away from interactions with the sources. For example, consistent discipline has its effect because it provides objective control conditions, namely contingency; intrusive parents may undermine control because they lower contingencies and reduce children's action. In a similar vein, actual "performance enactments" are a powerful influence on control (Bandura, 1977), because they are a source of credible information about all three elements. And vicarious experience is a source of information not only about the effective enactment of strategies but also about objective contingencies, such as what will happen when a snake is held. Likewise, verbal persuasion can be aimed at capacity ("you can do it"), contingency ("this is how"), or action ("just do it").

In principle, these three mechanisms should be useful in analyzing the sources of control in any domain and any age level. They seem to work well as a post hoc strategy for explaining why some interventions have been effective in increasing control and others haven't; because some have attended to all the elements and some have neglected one or more (see Chapter 11). However, the real test is prospective, in identifying the features of the social context that promote or undermine control expectations in a relatively comprehensive way.

## Elements of Structure Versus Chaos

So far, we have been working mainly in the classroom context, and some in parenting, and tried to operationalize the elements of structure from the points of view of children and adults (see Table 6.1). We also developed a scheme for coding classroom interactions. We have tried to consider all three pathways by which social contexts can promote (or undermine) control experiences: (a) maximizing objective control conditions, by both setting up objective connections between means and ends (contingency) and ensuring that the individual has the resources to operate contingencies (help); (b) encouraging action (expectations); and (c) contributing to interpretations of performance that suggest the possibility of future control (translations) (see Figure 6.1). The ongoing struggle with

**TABLE 6.1** Items Tapping Children's and Adults' Perceptions of
Involvement and Structure From Teachers and Parents

|  | *Involvement* | *Structure* |
| --- | --- | --- |
| **Parent Provision** | | |
| *Child Report* | | |
| positive | My parents enjoy the time they spend with me. | My parents always do what they say they are going to do. |
| negative | My parents just don't understand me. | My parents keep changing the rules. |
| *Parent Report* | | |
| positive | I enjoy the time I spend with my child. | Before I ask something new of my child, I make sure he/she can handle it. |
| negative | Sometimes my child is hard to like. | When my child does something wrong, my reaction is not very predictable. |
| **Teacher Provision** | | |
| *Child Report* | | |
| positive | My teacher cares about how I do. | My teacher tells us what will happen when we break the rules. |
| negative | My teacher doesn't know me very well. | Every time I do something wrong, my teacher acts differently. |
| *Teacher Report* | | |
| positive | This student is easy to like. | I talk with this student about my expectations for him/her. |
| negative | I don't understand this student very well. | I find it hard to be consistent with this student. |

assessment will be used to illustrate issues in the analysis of struc-
ture (for details, see Belmont, Skinner, Wellborn, & Connell, 1988;
Regan & Skinner, 1993; Skinner & Regan, 1991; Wellborn, Connell,
Skinner, & Pierson, 1988).

*Contingency.* Following the work on learned helplessness, *contingency* is a description of the context's contribution to the connection
between an individual's efforts and desired and undesired outcomes (Seligman, 1975). Social agents can determine contingencies
in many different ways. In family contexts, the desired and undesired outcomes are often the behaviors of the parents themselves, so

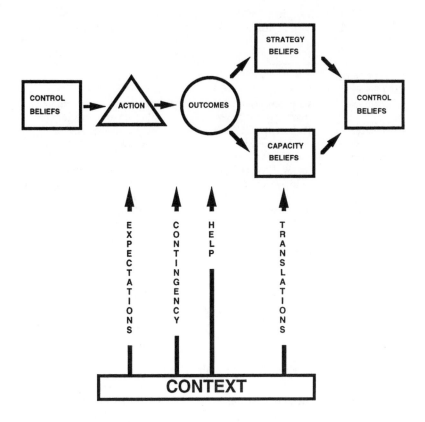

**Figure 6.1.** The Connections Between the Elements of Structure and the Competence System

contingency is the extent to which parents interpret correctly and respond consistently to children's bids and signals. In a parallel fashion, doctors may be differentially responsive to patient requests and input; supervisors to employees; spouses to each other. Social agents can also set contingencies. Teachers decide whether grades are based on participation, correctness of work, or neatness. Institutional caregivers reward compliance or independence.

Some setting of contingencies is less direct. For example, in classroom and work contexts, the contingency between action and outcome is often determined by task constraints, the foremost of which are task difficulty or workload, and time or deadlines. If a teacher assigns a task that is too difficult, a child will experience no contingency between action and outcome, no matter how much effort is exerted. If a boss requires a particular outcome, but does not allow the employee enough time to produce it successfully, the employee experiences noncontingency. A key to offering contingency is the provision of tasks and materials that respond to the actions of which the person is currently capable (or almost capable).

Sometimes the source of contingencies in a context is not any one person, or even people at all. The application of physical laws and the laws of chance are the clearest example. Even in social organizations, contingencies are not always under direct control of one individual. When business conditions deteriorate, bosses are forced to fire workers who are doing their jobs well. Teachers cannot provide sufficient attention to individual students when classes are too large. Doctors cannot guarantee the success of a treatment for cancer. Nevertheless, even when contingencies are not set by people, they can be described and their effects on perceived control examined.

In our observations in schools, we found it useful to distinguish three sources of contingencies: task-based (where performance is the outcome), rule-based (where discipline is the outcome), and interpersonal (where the behavior of another person is the target outcome) (see also Dweck et al., 1978; Pintrich & Blumenfeld, 1985). In the classes we observed, there was little variation among students in the amount of interpersonal structure they experienced from their teachers; it was uniformly high. However, a great deal of the structure in the classrooms was carried by rule-based contingencies. The physical environment provided structure, by the arrangement of chairs, the bells that ended periods, the way children walked to recess and even to the rest rooms. Rules were everywhere; they were explained very early in the school year (usually the first day) and constituted a highly salient background that didn't need much direct teacher behavior to bring into foreground; often a look or blinking the lights was all that was needed. In addition, the most salient contingencies were task-based; they were provided by the responsiveness of the academic material itself, of the math problems and spelling words, to the child's efforts to learn or solve them.

*Help.* Contexts can increase the resources available to produce desired outcomes by intervening directly into action episodes. Providing resources needed to operate contingencies is referred to as *help.* Help can range from taking over and completing a task to simply monitoring a task when it is completed. Help also includes information about how to deploy existing resources, such as strategy provision, direct training, and meta-cognitive or self-regulatory suggestions.

Although all the components of structure change in both their expression and their effects with development, age changes seem most pronounced in the effects of help on the experience of control. At very young ages, children think it reasonable to "send" an adult's hand to reach for something high on a shelf or for an adult to keep the bottom blocks steady while they themselves balance the upper ones. These direct interventions (sometimes called *scaffolding*; Wood, 1980) serve to increase the child's successful range of action and so increase control experiences. As children become older, however, it becomes more tricky to provide the kinds of help they can accept, without having it interfere with control experiences (Geppert & Kuester, 1983). This balancing act reaches its natural conclusion in the experience of caregivers attempting to help the frail elderly without undermining their control (Abeles, 1991; Karuza, Rabinowitz, & Zevon, 1986).

*Expectations.* The contextual dimension that increases the probability of action directly is summarized in the term *social expectations.* Expectations for successful action, studied for example in the work on self-efficacy (Bandura, 1986), can be communicated by a wide variety of sources. Verbal expectations include instructions, direct orders, and requests. Emotional displays also communicate expectations: impatience, surprise, and disappointment in response to behavior show that expectations are not being met. Some expectations are implicit and are only expressed directly when violated. These include norms, standards for behavior, family or classroom rules, and previously agreed upon responsibilities. Some are communicated through repetition and habit: Predicted rituals become expectations. Some are communicated through the behavior of the social agents; it is implied that the individual is expected to behave like everyone else, to conform. Expectations can be expressed by an absence of behavior as well: If a teacher does not call on a student or does not wait for a him to respond to a question, it is clear that she does not expect him to know the answer.

Expectations for action show distinct age grades. The elderly, just like patients in medical settings, are expected to be more passive, reflective, and withdrawn (Kuhl, 1986; Taylor, 1979). In fact, the institutionalized elderly receive social reinforcement contingent upon their passivity and compliance with staff (Baltes & Reisenzein, 1986). Although effective in producing desired social outcomes in institutions, norms and pressures for passivity at any age are developmentally dangerous, because they lead to disuse and eventual decline in skills and actual functioning (Kuhl, 1986), as has been shown in both physical and cognitive aging research.

*Translation.* The least precise subcomponent of structure is *translation*, which refers to the contribution of the social context to the interpretation of control episodes. These have been studied in detail by attribution researchers, as the proximal causes of attributions of outcomes to different kinds of causes, such as luck, effort, or ability. Like the other components, translations can be expressed through many channels: verbal, emotional, and task assignments. Verbal translations often take the form of attributions made by the social partners for the target individual's performance (e.g., "You sure were lucky" "Boy, you're really good at that" "Why can't you try harder?"). The chaotic form of translations can also be explicit ("You'll never do it" "Don't try that, it's too hard for you" "You blew it"). Even when not directly discussing the target individual's performances, social agents can emphasize the impossibility of personal control.

Emotions are also powerful communications of how the social context understands a performance. For example, following a child's failure, a teacher's sympathy communicates the uncontrollable cause of ability, whereas annoyance implies the more controllable cause of effort (Barker & Graham, 1987; Graham, 1984). Translations are also expressed through the organization of the physical environment. For example, a worker understands that if he fails and the boss assigns him another task of equal or greater difficulty, then she does not question his ability.

Social translations can also be seen as patterns of interactions over time. They often include contingencies and action outcomes as part of the process (Heckhausen, 1982; Skinner & Schmitz, 1994). For example, in elementary school, gender differences in ability estimates were not a function of differences in absolute level of critical teacher feedback about academic aspects of task performance. Instead, they were based on differences in relative patterns, such that the high amount of criticism boys regularly received for nonacademic aspects of work and conduct "diluted" the effects of the criticism on perceived ability (Dweck & Goetz, 1978).

## Conclusion

Understanding the facilitation of control experiences involves analyzing objective control conditions; how conditions are acted on to produce interactions with tasks, people, and institutions; and how those interactions are interpreted by the person and their social partners. Many elements must be in place for people to experience themselves as effective. However, if any one element is absent, then so too may be the experience of control. If the probability of action or outcome is zero or the actual contingencies are low, then no control experiences may be generated. And even if outcomes are actually produced contingently, the translation process may prevent them from being experienced as control.

This means that studies of contexts that undermine control can focus on the negative pole of any single element of structure, such as failure, noncontingency, or low expectations, and observe how it undermines control. Conversely, researchers who attempt either to assess or to intervene in order to *promote* control experience are struck by the range of changes in contexts and individuals that are needed. A thorough understanding of the competence system will require the identification, conceptually and empirically, of all the necessary conditions for the positive experience of control.

**PART IV**

# Consequences
# of Perceived Control

# Why Does Perceived Control Predict Everything?

Control is interesting to social scientists because of its simple appeal to everyday phenomenology and because it works in predicting a wide variety of mental and physical health outcomes. Reviews of constructs like locus of control (Strickland, 1989), self-efficacy (Bandura, 1989), or personal control (Rodin, Timko, & Harris, 1985) list literally dozens of psychological, social, and biological advantages associated with higher perceived control. A better understanding of the current pattern of correlates, as well as predictions in new domains and age groups, requires some specification of the reasons. Simply stated: When, where, how, and why does perceiving control result in adaptive outcomes? Recent research has provided some surprising insights into both the pathways and the phenomenological experience of control (for reviews, see especially, Bandura, 1989; Dweck, 1991; H. Heckhausen, 1991; Kuhl, 1984).

## When Does Perceived Control Work?

If perceiving control is such a universal human experience, it may seem surprising that, although people have thousands of contingency experiences every day, they do not usually spend much time reflecting on them. If perceptions of control are so central to psychological functioning, why don't people experience themselves perceiving control on a daily, if not hourly, basis? In general, perceived control remains in the background until people encounter obstacles, novelty, failure, noncontingency, uncertainty, stress, or the unexpected (Bandura & Schunk, 1981; H. Heckhausen, 1991; Weiner, 1985b). Perceived control can be experienced as foreground when the competence system is taxed. Much is known about the conditions under which this takes place.

*Changing Contingencies.* A burden is placed on the competence system in new situations, especially when old beliefs about how to reach goals and about the capacities of the self are not equal to producing desired outcomes. At a micro level, control beliefs are likely to be spontaneously experienced (and have been captured using talk-aloud protocols) in novel situations or ones characterized by failure and/or unexpected outcomes (Diener & Dweck, 1978; Weiner, 1985b).

At a more macro level of analysis, the effects of perceived control should be apparent as individuals approach and engage in novel activities, such as starting school, moving to a new neighborhood, beginning a new job, bringing home a new baby, planning retirement, or entering a nursing home. These are contexts in which old strategies may not apply and the discovery of new ones is apt to be filled with false starts and mistakes. Perceived control is likely to be especially salient if initial attempts to engage in effective interactions in these contexts do not produce intended outcomes. This analysis is consistent with a body of empirical work that shows the marked effects of perceived control during times of transition (Connell & Furman, 1984).

*Changing Competencies.* The competence system is also taxed when individuals undergo rapid changes in resources needed to operate contingencies. For example, the early preschool years are a period of rapid motor, cognitive, and social development. Issues of competence and control are at the surface of children's behavior during this time of rapid change, and so they are also at the surface of parents and children's interactions about the expression of those competencies ("I can *do* it!") (Dunn, 1988; Heckhausen, 1988).

At the other end of the life span, changes in competencies are also the rule. Although not as dramatic, they can be personally more salient because they usually involve decrements in functioning. Especially in the domains of health and cognition, the elderly experience intra-individual declines in robustness, resilience, and reserve (Baltes & Baltes, 1990; Brandtstaedter, Wentura, & Greve, 1993; Lachman, 1993). Consistent with this description, research has documented the important role of perceived control, especially in the domains of health and cognition, in the physical and psychological well-being of the elderly (Baltes & Baltes, 1986; Lachman, 1986b; Langer & Rodin, 1976; Nelson, 1990; Rodin et al., 1985; Schulz, 1976).

Other times of changing competencies may not be marked by specific age gradations (Baltes, 1987; Gurin & Brim, 1984). Accidents and changes in health status, even when the medical condition has been resolved, can produce lingering questions about the new or recovered competencies of the individual. Also salient would be setbacks in achievement domains, such as school failure or involuntary job termination. Losses of any kind, whether personal or social, may provoke a reassessment of control (Folkman, 1984).

## How Does Perceived Control Work?

Perceived control predicts a wide range of important outcomes across the domains of health, sports, school, work, marriage, and general life satisfaction. One way of organizing the range of outcomes that have been documented in the voluminous literature, as well as identifying life areas and outcomes that should *not* be affected by perceived control, would be to analyze the pathways by which beliefs have an impact on these diverse outcomes.

The basic argument of this chapter is that the primary psychological mechanism by which perceived control influences outcomes is through its effects on *action* and *action regulation*. Although these phenomena have been studied under many construct names (see Wellborn, 1991), the label most commonly used to refer to action is *motivation*, and to action regulation is *coping*. I am willing to argue that all of the psychological effects of perceived control can be traced back to these sources. Before this argument is explicated, one qualifier should be noted.

*Physiological Effects of Uncontrollability.* There is no question that the effects of perceived control are played out on the biological plane. Several decades of research have demonstrated the physiological damage, some permanent, caused by prolonged exposure to loss of control. In some species, perhaps in humans as well, the long-term result is death (Seligman, 1975). These effects seem to accrue through impairment of endocrine and immune system functioning. The importance of these psychoneuroimmunological effects is clear, especially when considering the effects of control on health outcomes (for reviews, see Gunnar, 1986, 1989; Kiecolt-Glaser & Glaser, 1990; Rodin, 1986; Rodin et al., 1985). However, although their importance is acknowledged, they will not be included in the following discussion, which instead will focus on the *psychological* effects of perceived control.

*Definition of Motivated Action.* Following an action theoretical perspective, action is defined as intentional goal-directed behavior. Accordingly, action consists of three interrelated components: behavior, orientation, and emotion (Connell & Wellborn, 1991; Wellborn, 1991). Perceived control does not influence every aspect of the components of action, only those that reflect motivation and volition.

*Behavior.* The motivational aspects of behavior have received the most attention as the proximal outcomes of perceived control. When people believe they can exercise control over important outcomes, they will initiate responses, try out strategies, exert effort, persist, and in general, behave actively. In contrast, when people believe they have no control, they will remain passive, not exert themselves, and give up easily.

*Orientation.* A motivated orientation refers to outlook, to the direction of action (Harter, 1978; Kuhl, 1981). When perceived control is high, a person tends to orient *toward* the activity, attending to it, focusing on it, acting on it, observing it, interacting actively with it. An orientation toward competence experiences leads people to select tasks at the border of their competencies, to set high goals, to plan, to prefer novel, puzzling, and unfamiliar situations, to embrace challenges. When perceived control is low, people tend to move away from challenges: They prefer easy and familiar tasks; they shy away from difficult situations; they avoid novelty; they decline opportunities to exercise or expand competencies; during task performance they are distracted by other things.

*Emotion.* The "motivated" aspects of emotion include positive feelings, such as interest, curiosity, enthusiasm, pride, happiness, satisfaction, and joy; as well as negative ones, such as anxiety, fear, sadness, embarrassment, guilt, and anger. Most motivational theories that have considered emotional consequences of perceived control have done so in a relatively undifferentiated way. That is, they show that low control produces general negative emotions, such as anxiety (Bandura, 1977), or positive mood (Affleck, Tennen, Pfeiffer, & Fifield, 1987).

The two exceptions are attributional theories. Reformulated learned helplessness theory has focused on one emotion, depression, and tried to detail all the aspects of perceived control that influence it (Peterson & Seligman, 1984). A complementary approach has been taken in Weiner's theory of causal attributions. A central goal has been to provide a differentiated picture of the kinds of causal understandings responsible for a wide range of emotions (Weiner, 1985a). Attributional perspectives have also been quite successful in tracing age differences in the patterns of attributions that lead to certain emotions (Graham, 1984).

## Why Does Perceived Control Work?

Why do people with low control give up, prefer easy tasks, feel anxious? For many decades, it was assumed that the answer to questions about mechanisms was obvious and straightforward. If one believes one has no control, then it is rational not to try; and lack of effort will undermine performance. Hence, explanations were motivational (see H. Heckhausen, 1991, for a review). However, recent research on volition (Heckhausen & Gollwitzer, 1987), action versus state orientation (Kuhl, 1984), self-regulation (Bandura, 1989), and goals (Dweck, 1991) has expanded our understanding of the mechanisms involved, revealing that they are more various, pervasive, and insidious than previously imagined.

An action sequence can be used to identify the points at which perceived control can impede performance (Chapman & Skinner, 1985; Dweck & Elliott, 1983; H. Heckhausen, 1991). Usually considered are task selection, goal setting, planning, intention formation, action initiation, action implementation, and evaluation. The effects described below have been found both as individual characteristics and as general reactions to prolonged situations of failure, noncontingency, and chaos (for reviews see Bandura, 1989; Berry & West, 1993; Dweck & Elliott, 1983; H. Heckhausen, 1991).

People with high control select challenging tasks. When they imagine task scenarios, they envision an interesting and fun process of interaction and successful outcomes (Bandura, 1989). People with high control tend to set high and concrete goals, which facilitate performance (Schunk, 1990). They have more organized, elaborated, and structured representations of the action space (Skinner, in press) and can imagine more means-ends connections leading to desired outcomes. They are able to visualize a concrete series of action steps leading to the desired outcome.

As a result, people with high control construct more effective action plans and exert more sustained effort in their enactment. Research on volition also suggests that people with high control are more likely to show an "action orientation," which gives them access to more of their own cognitive resources during action implementation (H. Heckhausen, 1991; Kuhl, 1984). During action, people with high control are able to focus their attention on a "fully developed action structure"; this allows them to concentrate completely on the task at hand (selective attention and encoding), to have full access to their working memory capacity (information processing), and to boost their intentions in the face of obstacles (determining emotions) (Kuhl, 1984). As a result, they show a pattern of more effective strategy selection, hypothesis testing, problem-solving, and general analytic thinking (Bandura, 1989; Dweck, 1991). In addition, when actions do not initially succeed, people with high control are more likely to increase effort exertion and persist, but also to adapt and revise action plans to match existing conditions.

People who do not expect control set low and diffuse goals. Their representations of the action space are disorganized, truncated, and chaotic, containing few means-ends relations (Skinner, in press). They do not spontaneously visualize sequential action steps. When prospectively reflecting on an activity, they imagine a process full of anxiety, culminating in failure outcomes (Bandura, 1989). As a result, people with low control show a "state orientation." When faced with action implementation, they have only "degenerated intentions," action plans that are tentative, conditional, and to which commitment is lacking (Kuhl, 1981). They continue to deliberate about the likelihood of failure, to wonder whether successful action is possible, and to ruminate about the consequences of failure (Deiner & Dweck, 1978). These degenerated intentions use up working memory capacity, distract attention, interfere with concentration, siphon off energy, and create intruding emotions. As a result, people have less actual capacity available to them in the implementation of action. In contrast to motivational deficits, these are referred to as *functional deficits* (Kuhl, 1981).

People with low and high control do not have opposite but equal experiences. When selecting tasks, people with low control choose tasks that are extremely easy or extremely hard, so that performance cannot be used to diagnose ability (H. Heckhausen, 1991). However, people with high control do not select tasks that are relatively difficult in order to diagnose their competence (even though success on these tasks does imply high ability). Instead, they do not seem to focus on demonstrating or evaluating high ability at all; they are focused on the task (Dweck & Leggett, 1988; Nicholls, 1984). They select challenging tasks because they seem to be the most interesting and fun.

When confronted by setbacks or failure, children and adults with low control actively wonder about their efficacy, doubt the controllability of the task, feel confused, and imagine the consequences of failure. In contrast, children and adults with high perceived control do *not* spend time reflecting about their high control, their positive abilities, or their probable success (Dweck & Leggett, 1988). They are engrossed in the task itself. That is how the competence system is designed to function, to carry one into interesting activities, fully focused on learning how to produce effects. Only after interactions are completed will beliefs be used to evaluate action episodes and make decisions about future goals and actions (H. Heckhausen, 1991).

## Where Does Perceived Control Work?

Most researchers in the area of perceived control agree that control beliefs have an impact on people's action and action regulation. In fact, they have been arguing this point for decades. What is controversial about the current position is the insistence that *all* psychological consequences of control are mediated by action, that is, that perceived control exerts effects *only* on outcomes that are influenced by action. This argument has two important implications. First, it alerts researchers to possible pathways through which perceived control can come to be correlated with outcomes. Second, from this analysis we can conclude that perceived control only improves outcomes within the constraints of actual control, that is, actual contingencies and competence. How does this translate into the contributions of control to functioning in different areas of life?

*Action Only.* If all of the broad-ranging psychological effects of perceived control are carried out through the medium of action, then conceptual and empirical life is simplified. The daunting task of analyzing the important components of perceived control in a particular domain is reduced to examining motivational and volitional effects of profiles of control on action and its organization. For example, in all domains, control would be expected to have a direct positive effect on task selection, planning, and goal-setting activities, and it would be expected to have a direct beneficial influence on the experience of positive emotions, like interest, fun, satisfaction, and joy, with resultant lower levels of emotional distress. Because of its volitional effects, it should have special impact in activities requiring high levels of cognitive processing capacity.

Motivational effects would be apparent in domain-specific manifestations of engagement. For example, in the classroom, perceived control has proximal effects on task orientation, studying, effort, attention, classroom participation, and use of meta-cognitive and self-regulatory strategies (Berry & West, 1993). In the domain of work, effects of perceived control would be expected to be strongest on job and occupational involvement, absenteeism, disrupted performance, and job satisfaction (Hoff & Hohner, 1986; Remondet & Hansson, 1993). In relationships, control should predict indicators of relationship engagement and involvement. In sports, it would have its primary impact on preparation, practice, and intensity of effortful participation in sports events; people with low control are likely to avoid voluntary sports activities and to engage in them minimally when they cannot be avoided. Perceived control should increase elderly people's enthusiastic involvement in the activities they value. In health, the strongest positive effects of perceived control would be seen on compliance and participation in treatments and health care regimes that patients expect to be effective; other effects could also be observed on patients' health-related choices, such as use of elective medical procedures, living wills, and unconventional medical treatments (Kaplan, 1991).

*Constraints of Actual Contingencies.* Because the effects of perceived control are mediated by action, it should have no *direct* effects on level of successful outcomes, like objective physical health, job success, promotion and pay, academic success, sports wins, or relationship longevity. The magnitude of the effects is constrained by actual contingencies between individual action and level of outcome in the respective domains. For example, in the work domain, the effects of perceived control would be limited to those that could be influenced by an individual's engagement in his or her job; no matter how much effort a person exerts in a low-paying child-care position, he or she will not change the pay scale for those jobs. In a similar vein, the psychological effects of perceived control on *objective* physical health depend on the extent to which that aspect of physical health can actually be influenced by patient participation. To put it simply, perceived control can predict consistent taking of medication; it cannot influence the extent to which the medication is effective in alleviating the medical condition.

*Constraints of Actual Competence.* A focus on action as the "only" psychological outcome of control also makes clear that, although perceiving control may increase one's future competencies through its effects on practice, it doesn't add to one's actual current talent or ability. It doesn't make basketball players taller or increase school children's genetic endowment of intelligence. It simply gives people access to all the resources they already have, to all the responses in their repertoire. For example, children with high control are more likely to show cognitive performances closer to the optimal performance of which they are capable (Chapman et al., 1990; Schmitz & Skinner, 1993). Hence, the effects of action on outcomes are limited by the actual competence of the individual. As a result, the effects of perceived control should be greatest where actual competence is already present, that is, for people whose existing repertoires are intact, but who are not expressing the behaviors, or in situations in which responses needed to operate contingencies are in everyone's repertoire already. This has been shown to be the case, for example, with phobics and with compliance to exercise regimes (Bandura, 1977).

## Conclusion

In sum, beliefs about control become phenomenologically salient when the competence system is taxed. Challenges to the competence system are provided by novel and unexpected situations, by mistakes or failure, and by changing individual competencies. The psychological effects of control are played out through motivation and volitional effects on action and its regulation, including task selection, goal setting, planning, intention formation, action initiation, action implementation, and evaluation. If action is the primary, or even the only, proximal psychological consequence of perceived control, does it follow then that the effects of the construct are quite limited, despite claims of its proponents? No. The reason that perceived control does indeed have an impact on such a wide range of outcomes is that motivation and volition are critical factors underlying every performance that depends on effortful behavior for success. Hence, low perceived control can always prevent people from performing at the peak of their capacities; it increases the chances of failure, and can even prevent them from attempting a task at all. However, high perceived control does not guarantee success. Instead, its effects are constrained by actual contingencies in the situation and existing competencies of the individual.

# 8

## How Does Perceived Control
## Work During Times of Stress?

From the enormous literature on the benefits of control, it is easy to conclude that perceived control should be a powerful ally in times of stress. In fact, in research on stress, objective uncontrollability and unpredictability are considered noxious events, requiring adaptation from the organism (Garmezy, 1983; Miller, 1979; Rodin, 1986). In the study of psychological resources for coping, perceived control has been found to buffer stress for children (Compas, 1987; Compas, Banez, Malcarne, & Worsham, 1991), adults (Folkman, 1984; Lefcourt, 1982), and the elderly (Rodin et al., 1985). In his review of the early work, Lefcourt (1982) suggested that, "evidence has been found that resourcefulness and resilience in encounters with stressful experience reflect the belief held by individuals that they are responsible agents who are at least partially responsible for what befalls them" (p. 102). In sum, "Control, perceived and actual, matter in the way persons wrestle with life's adversities" (p. 110).

However, as observed by many authors (including Lefcourt), research on the effects of control, and especially experimental work, does not always map onto the central issues of coping with stress.

First, the magnitude of stressors to be dealt with are different. As noted by Thompson and colleagues,

> the types of events to which experimental participants can be subjected . . . pale in comparison with the intensity and potential impact of "real world" stressors . . . loss of a loved one, diagnosis . . . of a serious chronic illness, or being the victim of a crime are the types of events that can arouse concerns about issues of control and mastery in ways that are more intensive and extensive than the laboratory presentation of stressful situations. (Thompson, Sobolew-Shubin, Galbraith, Schwankowsky, & Cruzin, 1993, p. 293)

As opposed to single stressors used in the lab, during real life traumatic events, people are faced not only with the "event" itself, such as rape, diagnosis of cancer, divorce, or loss of a parent, but also with a host of consequences that may themselves become the target of control efforts (Folkman, 1984). The time frame is also different; coping is usually considered to be a process that unfolds over time, sometimes years (Folkman & Lazarus, 1985). Further, during the process of coping, the relations between control and coping are likely to be reciprocal. Control influences coping reactions, but control itself may also change as a function both of the occurrence of the negative event and based on the extent to which the stressor yields to attempts to modify it.

Compared to the lab, the array of reactions to real life stress are also much wider, including more intense emotions, such as depression and loneliness, and more heterogeneous behaviors, such as escape, opposition, or help-seeking (Garmezy & Rutter, 1983). In stressful situations in real life, it is also much more difficult to specify a priori what patterns of coping are adaptive. In the lab, it has been assumed that problem-focused, persistent, active attempts to ameliorate the problem are beneficial. However, coping theorists point out that such reactions may be maladaptive in circumstances that are objectively uncontrollable (such as in a terminal illness) and may lead to frustration and exhaustion, or may exacerbate feelings of powerlessness (Compas et al., 1991; Folkman, 1984; Weisz, 1983).

A needs theory of competence provides an original framework for ordering thorny issues in the conceptualization of stress, coping,

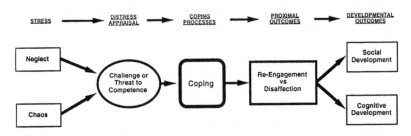

**Figure 8.1.** A Simple Process Model of the Relations Between Social Context, Self, Coping, and Developmental Outcomes
SOURCE: Adapted from Skinner & Wellborn, 1994.

and control (Skinner & Wellborn, 1994). It can be a useful basis to differentiate objective stress from subjective distress, to specify the kinds of stress for which perceived control can (and cannot) act as a psychological buffer, and to provide hypotheses about the mechanisms by which perceived control influences coping and adaptive outcomes. It can be especially useful in identifying a range of responses to stress and specifying when they will have adaptive developmental consequences. The theory of stress and coping described in this chapter is part of a larger conceptualization that incorporates not only the need for competence, but also for relatedness and autonomy (Skinner & Wellborn, 1994). An overview of the competence portion of the model is presented in Figure 8.1.

## A Needs Analysis of Coping

*Stress and Distress.* One thing that all stress researchers agree on is that there is no consensus about definitions of stress (Rutter, 1983). Some psychological theories of coping define it as a state of mind. For example, Lazarus and Folkman (1984) define stress as "a particular relationship between the person and the environment that is appraised by the person as taxing or exceeding his or her resources and endangering his or her well-being" (p. 19). The difficulty with subjective definitions is that in examining the differential effects of stress, it is impossible to know whether one is assessing the effects of differentially taxing circumstances or the effects of differential *vulnerability* to situations of equal difficulty.

A needs theory allows for the separation of objective from subjective stress. Objectively stressful to the competence system is *chaos*. Described fully in Chapter 6, chaos includes noncontingency, unpredictability, actual uncontrollability, normlessness, confusion, and novelty. These features of situations can be assessed independently of an individual's estimates of them. In fact, stress research on the effects of objective noncontingency, unpredictability, and actual loss of control have succeeded, not only in operationalizing these elements of chaos, but separating them from each other, and demonstrating that each does in fact place demands on the organism (Gunnar, 1980; Levine, 1983; Seligman, 1975; Weinberg & Levine, 1980).

If differential vulnerability to stress is also of interest, then in addition to an objective definition, a perspective on the individual's reaction to the situation is also required. As noted by many stress researchers, a difficult task may be experienced by one person as a crushing burden and by another as an interesting challenge. Although controversial when introduced, the notion that individuals' appraisals of the situation influence their coping is now widely accepted (Lazarus & Folkman, 1984). Consistent with this position, we define *distress* as the subjective experience that a need (in this case, for competence) is being impinged upon.

Following the typology of Lazarus and Folkman (e.g., 1984), events relevant to the competence system can be appraised as (a) *challenges* to competence, producing reactions that are active, positive, and oriented toward the event, aimed at restoring or replenishing the need for competence; (b) *threats* to competence, producing reactions that are emotionally negative, active, and oriented toward escaping the situation, aimed at fighting for the need; and (c) *losses* of competence, producing reactions that are negative, passive, and oriented away from the situation, aimed at protecting the self from the impact of the assault to the need. Finally, events that are not experienced as impinging on the competence system (or any other need) would be appraised as benign, neutral, or irrelevant.

For example, in operationalizing this distinction in the academic domain for children, we tapped threat appraisals with items like

"When I do badly on an important test, I feel stupid," "When I can't answer a question in class, I feel like an idiot," and "When I run into a problem I can't solve on a test, I know I will miss all the other ones, too" (Skinner & Wellborn, 1992). These appraisals are reminiscent of the processes discussed by Dweck (1991) in which children respond to failure with sweeping generalizations about the self; or described by attributional models of learned helplessness in which noncontingency is generalized across time (stability) and situations (globality). Following this work, there are no corresponding appraisals for challenge events. In these cases, children and adults tend not to reflect on their control.

*Coping.* Definitions and categories of coping are as varied as the disciplines from which coping theories have emerged (Skinner, Altman, Sherwood, Yoder, & Grossmann, 1994). The most common classification in research with both adults and children is problem-focused versus emotion-focused coping, or coping responses aimed at changing the stressor versus at dealing with one's own emotional reactions to it (Folkman & Lazarus, 1984). Research from this perspective has examined the connections between control and coping (see Compas et al., 1991, for a review). As would be expected, children and adults with higher perceived control also show more problem-focused coping. In general, studies have not found a connection between perceived control and level of emotion-focused coping. However, in other research, when individuals' beliefs about "thought control of action" are tapped directly, it seems that individual differences in self-efficacy for these activities predict more active and productive attempts to maintain positive affect and to terminate or divert negative, anxiety-provoking, depressing, and intrusive thoughts (Bandura, 1989).

We have approached this problem by conceptualizing coping as an organizational construct, which describes "how people regulate their own behavior, emotion, and orientation under conditions of psychological stress" (Skinner & Wellborn, 1994, p. 112). In general, action regulation refers to how people mobilize, guide, manage, energize, and direct their behavior, emotion, and orientation, or how they fail to do so (see also Eisenberg, Fabes, & Guthrie, in press; Kopp,

1982). This definition was used to construct a matrix of general coping categories, which can then be operationalized, based on their expression in different domains and age groups. For competence, these are depicted in Figure 8.2. The columns of the matrix are the three targets of regulation, behavior, emotion, and orientation. The rows cross the appraisals of (a) whether the situation presents a challenge versus a threat, and (b) whether the source of the challenge/ threat is the self or the context.

When a situation is seen as a challenge to the competence system stemming from the self, the individual determines to change the self to become more competent. This results in active attempts to discover how the contingencies in the context can be operated, through effort, strategizing, problem-solving, and experimentation. These behaviors are undertaken with the spirit of resolve, knowing that contingencies are available and mistakes can be repaired. When the source of a challenge to the competence system is seen, not as the self, but as the context, an individual responds with a determination to change the context to make it more controllable. The behaviors stemming from this appraisal are aimed at locating effective contingencies, and include information-seeking of all kinds, ranging from observation to consultation to reading. These behaviors are accompanied by an optimistic attitude and an outlook toward planning and preventing problems from occurring in the future.

These coping responses can be contrasted with those produced by appraisals that the competence system is threatened. When the source of the threat is viewed as the self, the individual feels incompetent. As a result, behaviors are lacking, emotions are full of self-doubt, and the general orientation is confusion. If, on the other hand, the context is seen as the source of the threat, then the individual experiences the environment as unpredictable and dangerous. In response, the individual attempts to escape, feeling hopeless, and in the future avoids or puts off the threatening activity as long as possible.

*Domain and Developmental Level Constraints on Coping.* The 12 coping responses shown in Figure 8.2, along with those generated by appraisals of challenge and threat to the relatedness and autonomy

**APPRAISALS**

**COPING RESPONSES**

| Source of Distress | Severity of Distress | | Regulation of Behavior | Regulation of Emotion | Regulation of Orientation |
|---|---|---|---|---|---|
| SELF | CHALLENGE | "I will learn." | Strategize | Resolve | Repair |
| | THREAT | "I am helpless." | Confusion | Self-doubt | Discouragement |
| CONTEXT | CHALLENGE | "I will reduce chaos." | Information-seeking | Optimism | Prevention |
| | THREAT | "The world is unpredictable." | Escape | Pessimism | Avoidance |

COMPETENCE

**Figure 8.2.** Coping Responses From Distress Appraisals Related to Competence
SOURCE: Adapted from Skinner & Wellborn, 1994.

84

systems, have been examined in children's open-ended interviews about their behaviors, emotions, and orientations in stressful situations in school and friendship interactions (Skinner, Altman, & Sherwood, 1993). To give a flavor of these responses, short descriptions of the categories relevant to competence are included in Table 8.1, along with examples from children's transcripts.

In attempting to chart coping during middle childhood in only two domains, academics and friendship, we were struck by the constraints placed on coping by both domain and developmental level. For example, when the global categories of coping were translated into a set of self-report items for children during middle childhood in the academic domain (Skinner & Wellborn, 1992; see Table 8.2), it became clear that one of the features of the context that shapes coping responses most strikingly is the power differential in relationships. "Escape" from a difficult exam does not include actually leaving the scene of the stressful incident. It is constrained by the context to "wishing" to escape or mental escape. When students are angry, they may feel like ripping up their textbooks, but usually do not. When they want to avoid something, like homework, they procrastinate. In response to conflicts and problems with friends, however, children are freer to directly express their coping: They can be more aggressive, they can walk away more from stressful situations, they can actively avoid others with whom they have problems (Skinner et al., 1993).

## Perceived Control and Structure as Psychological and Social Resources

Interventionists who wish to help individuals cope better are very interested in the issue of personal and social coping resources (Moos & Billings, 1982; Pearlin & Schooler, 1978). Among the wide range of factors that support coping responses, perceived control is often mentioned. For example, in the research on resilience in children, when children under great stress are divided into those who show severe psychological consequences and those who are functioning relatively well, level of perceived control consistently differentiates

**TABLE 8.1** Coding Categories for Coping Responses and Examples From Open-Ended Interviews

*Behavior Regulation*

1. *Strategizing:* Attempt or try alone; mental effort aimed at recall, remembering, thinking. Generate strategies, think about next action steps; actively decide about a series of behaviors, especially based on likelihood of reaching an outcome. "I tried to think 'What could the answer be?' " "I tried my hardest to get them right" "I thought about a way to . . ."

2. *Information-Seeking:* Gather new information from a source outside the self about contingencies, situational constraints, possible behaviors, strategies, capacities, or possible outcomes. "I read all I can about . ." "I ask them what they'd like to play" "I asked them what was wrong, why they were mad at me" "I asked my dad to explain the parts I didn't understand."

3. *Observation:* Look over situation and/or listen. "I watched them play" "I saw how she did it."

4. *Confusion:* General uncertainty about situation; not understanding or not being able to figure something out; absence of directedness of behavior. Uncertainty about next action steps or strategies. "I didn't understand what she was talking about" "I didn't know why she was so mad" "My mind goes blank" "I just didn't know what happened" "not sure what to do next."

5. *Passivity:* Not do anything; absence of behavior, includes low effort, not exerting energy or trying. "I just stood there" "I just sat there and pretended I listened" "I didn't do anything" (What did you do?) "Not really anything."

6. *Escape:* Remove oneself from the situation. Physically (e.g., get out of there, leave, go, take off) or mentally remove oneself; actively think about something else; distraction; daydream. Escape fantasies, wish situation or event were over or gone. "I just walked away" "I went home" "I thought about something else" "I felt like, 'When is this going to be over ?' " "I was thinking that if I were in New Jersey I could do whatever I want."

*Emotion Regulation*

1. *Resolve:* Determination to solve problem or reduce chaos or uncertainty. Attempts to persuade self that self has the capacity to produce a successful outcome. "I'll get to the bottom of this" "I'll figure this out" "I tell myself 'You can do it.' " "I say 'You can figure this out.' "

2. *Optimism:* Expectation of increasing probability of occurrence of positive events; positivism about the future, the next event, or the consequences of the current event; faith in positive outcomes. "I know it'll work out eventually" "I knew we'd make up in the end" "I felt that it'd probably be easier, the next spelling thing."

3. *Self-Doubt:* Worry, anxiety, or unease about events or situations. Wishing or wondering about current or future performance. "worry that I'll fail the test again" "I was thinking about whether I'd get it right or wrong" "I'd feel worried, 'cause if I didn't know lots of the words."

4. *Pessimism:* Expectation of negative events; negativism about the current situation or the future, or the next event. Anxiety or unease about the long-term conse-

quences of the event. Futility, "I know it won't work out" "I'll get it wrong anyway" "I knew we'd end up fighting" "I thought that I was probably gonna get lots of words wrong" "They'll never let me play."

*Orientation Regulation*

1. *Repair:* Attempt to undo or compensate for damage caused by the event; repairing practical and emotional consequences for self and others; apologizing and forgiving self and others. "I told her I was sorry" "I told her I would not do it again" "I redid it" "I gave a note to Kim to give to her" "I invited her to my birthday party."

2. *Prevention:* Attempt or decide to prevent a reoccurrence of events. Use event to learn something about self (e.g., capacities) or world (e.g., strategies). Key phrases: figure out what I did wrong, how this happened, what I learned. "Think of what I can learn from all this."

3. *Discouragement:* Desire to give up or stop trying. "I just don't want to do any more" "I want to give up" "I just don't feel like doing any more."

4. *Avoidance:* Prevent contact with person or situation that was negative in the past; ignoring. Put off contact with person or situation; wait until the last possible moment to begin an activity or make contact with a person. "I never ask them to play again" "I try not to take classes on that subject again" "I ignored her" "Just left each other alone" "I just walked by him" "I waited until the last minute."

SOURCE: Adapted from Skinner, Altman, & Sherwood, 1991.

those groups (Compas, 1987). Similarly, in studies of the elderly, perceived control was correlated with more adaptive coping (Duncan & Morgan, 1980; Rodin, 1980). Despite the finding that people with high control also show more adaptive coping with life stress, relatively little is known about the precise mechanisms by which perceived control should ameliorate the effects of stress (Folkman, 1984).

*Perceived Control as a Buffer.* A needs theory of competence suggests several pathways for both direct and indirect effects. First, perceived control provides protection against the experience of distress in times of elevated objective chaos. In other words, control has an effect on initial appraisals of stressfulness of an event (Folkman, 1984). High control prevents failure, mistakes, noncontingency, and novelty from being experienced as threats to the competence system, whereas low control increases an individual's vulnerability to the experience of chaos. Hence, high perceived control

**TABLE 8.2** Items Tapping Competence From the Coping Questionnaire in the Academic Domain

| Category | Item Example |
|---|---|
| **Appraisal** | |
| When something bad happens to me in school (like not doing well on a test or not being able to answer an important question in class), | |
| *Catastrophizing* | I worry that I'll never learn how to do it. |
| | I worry that I won't do well on anything. |
| *Self-Derogation* | I feel like the dumbest person in the world. |
| | I feel totally stupid. |
| **Behavioral Regulation** | |
| When I run into a problem on an important test, | |
| *Strategize* | I try to figure out what to do next. |
| | I try to think of different ways to do it. |
| *Confusion* | My mind goes blank. |
| | I'm not sure what to do next. |
| When I have trouble with a subject in school, | |
| *Information-Seeking* | I try to find out more about it. |
| | I try to understand the material better. |
| *Escape* | I wish we didn't have to do anymore. |
| | I wish we'd just stop working on it. |
| **Emotional Regulation** | |
| When I have trouble learning something, | |
| *Resolve* | It makes me want to try even more. |
| | It makes me want to work even harder. |
| *Self-Doubt* | I think to myself, "You're in over your head." |
| | I say to myself "This is just too hard for you." |
| When I run into a difficult problem on a test, | |
| *Optimism* | I can usually get it. |
| | After a minute, the answer comes to me. |
| *Pessimism* | I'll probably miss it. |
| | I won't figure out the answer. |
| **Orientation Regulation** | |
| When something bad happens to me in school (like not doing well on a test or not being able to answer an important question in class), | |
| *Repair* | I try to fix it. |
| | I try to make it better. |
| *Discouragement* | I want to give up. |
| | I feel like quitting. |
| When I have difficulty learning something, | |
| *Prevention* | I try to figure out how to do better next time. |
| | I try to figure out what to do so it won't happen again. |
| *Avoidance* | I put off working on it. |
| | I wait until the last minute to work on it. |

SOURCE: Adapted from Skinner & Wellborn, 1992.

ensures that one of the things that a person will *not* have to cope with is the negative reactions of the self.

As a second line of defense, control influences the way people cope when they do experience the demands of objective conditions as taxing to the competence system. In addition to its effects on individual coping responses, perceived control plays a role in maintaining the organization of action under stressful conditions (Eisenberg et al., in press; Maccoby, 1983) and ensuring that all cognitive resources are available (H. Heckhausen, 1991; Kuhl, 1984).

*Structure as Social Support.* Given how much is known about chaos as a stressor and perceived control as a personal resource, surprisingly little has been explicitly written about structure as a social resource that buffers the effects of stress (Grolnick & Bridges, 1993; Skinner & Wellborn, 1994). The aspects of structure that have been studied are described as some of the multiple facets of social support (Wellborn, 1993). Although the elements can be looked at individually, considering them all as different facets of the overarching construct of structure would allow a more unified theoretical approach to specifying the mechanisms and conditions under which structure buffers the effects of stress.

The needs model of competence can explain how these supports influence coping responses: through their effects on perceived control. It can also explain the kinds of stresses for which these supports will be especially helpful: when coping with events that are chaotic. Structure should not be helpful in situations where competence is not an issue (e.g., in situations that threaten relatedness or autonomy). Finally, it can explain the conditions under which these supports will not produce better coping: when they do not actually improve the experience of control. For example, the effects of instrumental aid in buffering stress have been especially difficult to document. Note the delicate balance needed to offer enough help to increase the probability of the outcome without undermining a sense of personal control (Karuza et al., 1986).

*Objective Stress.* Perceived control also has an indirect distal effect on coping through its effects on the probability of encounters with stress (Masten, 1994). Some stresses are externally generated: drug addicted parents, violence in the neighborhood, an irrational colleague, cancer, or job loss due to recession. But some stressful experiences are at least partially the product of individual behaviors: failure in school, trouble with the law, fights with peers. As pointed out by other researchers, the occurrence of these latter stressors can be reduced by perceived control and the coping and action it engenders (Duncan & Morgan, 1980). For example, one outcome of high perceived control is planning and more general attempts to produce good and prevent bad outcomes from occurring (Skinner, in press). Such planning has been shown to be a potent force in lessening the long-term negative consequences of harsh life circumstances (Rutter, 1989). In the health domain, individuals who show more health-maintenance and preventive behaviors will be sick less. At work, employees who show high job involvement and performance are less likely to be fired.

## Conclusion

Control influences coping through a variety of different pathways. People with high control act preemptively to prevent controllable stressful episodes from occurring; they appraise situations as less distressing when faced with chaos or difficulty. They have more of their resources available for focusing on the current situation, and they deploy them more readily to increase the contingencies in the context (through information-seeking or planning) or to increase the resources of the self (through strategizing, problem-solving, and learning). People with low control are likely to react to chaotic life events with distress caused by feelings of helplessness, to divert more resources toward managing that distress, and to use the resources that remain in a less focused and strategic manner. Taken together, these differential patterns of coping lead to qualitatively different phenomenological experiences of stress and also to different kinds of overt engagement with the stressful situation. These in turn should have effects on the resolution of the stressor. They should also determine whether the stressful episode has weakened the person's coping repertoire and rendered them more vulnerable to subsequent stresses, or has had a "steeling" effect, contributing to a more elaborated repertoire for coping with future problems and for effectively managing the self under stress.

**PART V**

# Development
# of Perceived Control

# 9

# How Do Individual Differences in Perceived Control Develop?

For most researchers interested in individual differences, the only developmental question that matters is, "Where did these individual differences come from?" If one assumes that after individual differences emerge, they crystallize and remain stable, then no more developmental issues need be explored. If, however, one assumes, as I do, that perceived control is a set of beliefs that not only guides action but also is open to revision based on experience and its interpretation, then stability, even if found empirically, must itself be explained. Hence, for developmentalists, the interesting question is, "Where do differences in these individual *trajectories*, in these patterns of change over time, come from?" (see Baltes, Reese, & Nesselroade, 1977).

In our own work, we have focused on the interaction between person and context, specifically on the effects of *experiences* of control on trajectories of beliefs. This work is based on the simple assumption that control beliefs and actions can create a self-perpetuating cycle (Seligman, 1975; Skinner, 1991a; see Figure 9.1). People who believe they have control act in ways that are more likely to produce

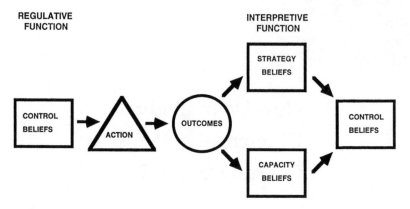

**Figure 9.1.** A Schematic of the Competence System, Including Control, Strategy, and Capacity Beliefs
SOURCE: Adapted from Skinner, 1991a.

success experiences, which then confirm their initial high estimates of control. High perceived control leads people to more objective contingency by selecting optimally challenging tasks, it encourages action, it offers performance interpretations that favor control, and over time, it even increases objective competence. In contrast, people who approach a task doubting whether they have a chance to succeed often act in ways that undermine control experiences, and these failures cement initial low expectations of control. Over time, this pattern of differential interactions will produce relative stability of perceived control. Depending on whether these beliefs-action-performance cycles confirm initial beliefs or lead to increments and decrements in control, this may be accompanied by magnification of initial individual differences in perceived control over time (see Figure 9.2).

This model can be tested at several levels. First, it should be consistent, not only with group differences, but also with the functioning of the competence system over time at the *individual* level. Second, individuals' trajectories of engagement should diverge over time and any given individual's trajectory should be predicted from both their initial level of beliefs and their individual trajectory of beliefs. In testing these hypotheses, we used two kinds of metho-

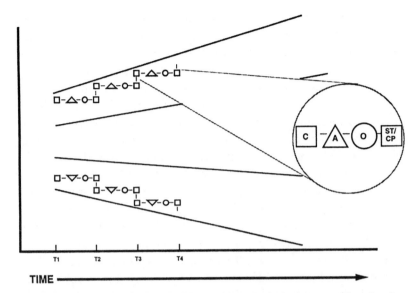

**Figure 9.2.** How Individual Differences Are Magnified Across Time by the Operation of the Competence System
SOURCE: Adapted from Skinner, 1991a.

dologies: an examination of intra-individual relations among control and action over time (Schmitz & Skinner, 1993), and the prediction of intra-individual trajectories of control beliefs and action (Skinner, Zimmer-Gembeck, & Connell, 1994). These two methods will be described in some detail because they may be useful in examining a range of phenomena relevant to the development of individual differences in the functioning of the competence system.

## The Cycle of Perceived Control and Action

Although each of the links in the functional model of perceived control has received ample empirical support in the literature to confirm it individually, few studies exist that attempt to examine all the links simultaneously as they unfold in their natural context. We set out to conduct such a study, looking for a setting in which children regularly exert effort to produce performance outcomes, and in which they know the success or failure of outcomes before engaging again in the task. We wanted to assess control and effort in relation to each performance cycle. Not surprisingly, we settled on the school context (see Schmitz & Skinner, 1993, for details).

Two basic questions were the focus of this work. First, does the model hold for explaining individual differences between children in daily functioning in a naturalistic context? Because performances were sequential, it was also possible, even in a naturalistic setting, to capture relations that indicate causal priority. Second, we wanted to examine the functional model at the *intra*-individual level. That is, can the model explain day-to-day variation within individuals? Intra-individual and interindividual questions are conceptually and empirically independent (Schmitz, 1987). For example, even though it is clear that as a group, people with high perceived control show greater effort exertion on difficult tasks, does this connection hold for individuals as well? That is, when a person believes he has more control, does he exert more effort on a subsequent difficult task (relative to when he believes he has less control)? It is possible that when a person estimates he has less control over an outcome he exerts more effort relative to when he believes control can be easily obtained. Interindividual and intra-individual data were used to examine each link in the model.

*Time Series Design.*   Data collection, which took place daily for about 4 months, was organized around children's graded assignments (homework and tests). Following the completion of each assignment but prior to grading, children reported on their action, both effort exertion and time spent either working on homework or studying for tests. Following the return of each graded assignment, children provided information about their actual performances, their subjective evaluation, and their attributions for their correct answers and errors to effort, ability, help, task difficulty, and unknown causes. Children also took a standard intelligence test and reported on their generalized beliefs about control. In addition, children provided information about some exploratory constructs that were not included in the model. The design is pictured in Figure 9.3.

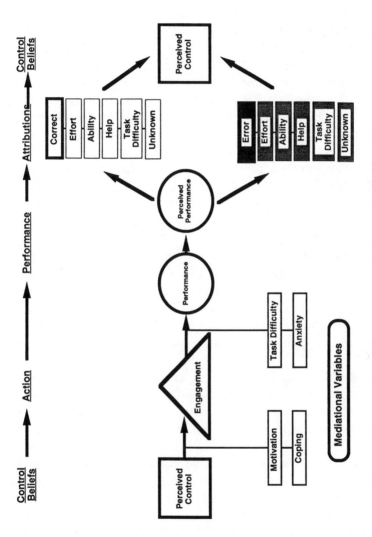

**Figure 9.3.** The Design of the Time Series Study of the Competence System

99

## Implications of Interindividual and Intra-Individual Analyses

Overall, the analyses of time series interindividual correlations supported the proposed model. Although interindividual findings were not surprising (because hypotheses were based on decades of interindividual research), it was useful to confirm predictions in a naturalistic context using sequential data that are consistent with a causal interpretation. We did expect that establishing the links in the model at the *intra-individual* level would prove less straightforward and more interesting. We were not disappointed on either count.

*Effort-Performance Contingency.* Most interesting, an intra-individual link that we assumed would be present for all children was not: the connection between amount of effort exerted and level of performance. We knew that the exertion-success link would be qualified by task difficulty and by intelligence; that is, difficult tasks require more effort and inhibit good performance, and smart children can try less and still do better than children who are not so smart. However, we assumed that, in general, for a given child, controlling for task difficulty, when she tries harder, she will do better. However, these links were not consistently present, and for some children, anxiety even produced a negative relation between effort and performance.

*Control-Effort Link.* Although in general children who expected higher control also exerted more effort, this connection was not found at the intra-individual level. In other words, when a child expected more control, he did not exert more effort on subsequent assignments (relative to times when he expected less control). Control boosted performance at the intra-individual level only for children who had the requisite coping skills or a more intrinsic motivation for the task.

An interesting interpretation for this finding is suggested by the high intra-individual stability of control expectations over the 4 months of the study. Perhaps children do not base their efforts on only the immediately previous control estimate. Perhaps they use a running total of experiences in deciding how much effort to exert. This possibility is consistent with the significant interindividual correlation between average daily control expectations (assessed in class) and generalized control beliefs (assessed using our questionnaire). Perhaps the use of a cumulative record of control experiences to regulate effort prevents active engagement from being derailed by a single failure experience.

*Performance, Attributions, and Control.* Although many similarities were found in the patterns of attributions for success and failure at the interindividual and intra-individual levels, the more interesting findings were differences between levels of analysis. These were especially striking for unknown and for effort attributions. In general, unknown control is one of the most maladaptive perceptions a student can have. Unknown control is a strong interindividual predictor of classroom disaffection, academic failure, and low achievement test scores (Connell, 1985). In the time series study, however, *more* successful students were likely to attribute their mistakes to unknown causes. Perhaps, on a daily basis and in the context of generally high performance, attributing the occasional mistake to unknown causes allows students not to dwell on their errors. It should be noted that, even at the intra-individual level, attributing *correct* answers to unknown causes is both more likely in the context of poor performance and leads to subsequently lower expectations of control. Hence, before incorporating this strategy into interventions, it deserves further study.

The same can be said for another attribution that is already included in many interventions into the competence system: attribution of errors to lack of effort. The pattern of findings at the intra-individual level does not support its assumed benign effects. First, at the intra-individual level, attributions of mistakes to effort are not connected with successful performances and do not lead to subsequently higher expectations of control (neither are they seen more often in failure nor do they lead to lower expectations). At the general level, however, interindividual analyses showed that average daily attributions of errors to effort is connected with poorer performance. Our interpretation for this finding is that, over the long run, poor performance accompanied by effort attributions may lead a child to believe that they cannot voluntarily regulate their effort (Skinner et al., 1990) or that they are not very smart (Covington & Omelich, 1985).

## Interindividual Differences in Change Over Time

One developmental goal of understanding the self-confirming cycle of beliefs and performance is to examine whether they produce differential developmental trajectories over time. The time frame for such developmental trajectories is not months, as in the time series study, but instead is years. We have just completed a longitudinal data collection of children's beliefs and performances in six waves over 3 years. In the analyses of these data, the target outcome will not be individual differences or developmental change; it will be individual differences in developmental change. Growth curves will be used to capture the concept of trajectories, and several strategies will be used to explore their antecedents and consequences (Connell & Skinner, 1990). Preliminary analyses look promising (Skinner, Zimmer-Gembeck, & Connell, 1994).

*Interindividual Differences in Change.* In this work, the target trajectory is children's engagement versus disaffection in classroom activities, and it is being predicted from children's profiles of control beliefs, both their initial level and their individual trajectories. Data are from about 360 children who have four consecutive measurement points, starting in the fall of an assessment year. We are also testing the possibility that both the shape of the engagement trajectories and their pattern of relations to control may differ for children of different ages. In this sample are children whose 2-year trajectories began in third through sixth grades.

Profile analysis has already determined that the general shape of the trajectories differs as a function of initial grade level. From a purely descriptive perspective, younger children's trajectories of engagement are basically high and stable, even gently increasing, whereas between fourth and fifth grade, they begin to decline. Strategy and capacity beliefs show a similar profile, when capacity beliefs are the average of beliefs about one's access to effort, ability, powerful others, and luck, and in which strategy beliefs are the combination of beliefs that effort is an important means for school performance and beliefs in ability, powerful others, luck, and unknown strategies are low. For all constructs, much variation in growth curves was apparent, both in initial level as well as shape, slope, and extent of change over the 2 years. The goal of growth curve analysis is to determine whether the differences in trajectories are systematically related to other constructs. We have been testing three possible models (Connell & Skinner, 1990).

*Predictors of Interindividual Differences in Change.* The first model, the *launch* model, assumes that variation in changes in children's engagement over time is a function of their initial differential starting levels of perceived control. The notion is that children who start off their experiences in school with optimistic beliefs will be more likely to engage more fully, leading to more subsequent success, higher control, and more engagement. In contrast, children who are initially pessimistic about school activities will become discouraged and increasingly withdraw from classroom participation over time. These hypotheses were tested by examining whether individual differences in children's engagement growth curves were systematically related to the initial level of their control beliefs.

The second model, referred to as the *change-to-change* model, looks at changes in engagement as a function of *changes* in children's perceptions of control. In this scenario, a child's active involvement in the classroom should mirror the shape of his or her perceived control, rising as it rises and falling as it falls. This model was tested by examining the relations between growth curves for engagement and perceived control.

A third model, the *ambient level* model, was not used to examine the relations between control and engagement but could be used to examine antecedents of both. This model tests whether individual differences in developmental change are due to the average level of support provided by the social context while the trajectory is unfolding. The notion is that a context rich in involvement and structure allows a child to increasingly engage in school activities, whereas one that is chaotic or neglectful would cause a child to become increasingly alienated from school over time. An initial high level of support would not be enough to ensure an optimal trajectory of engagement, so a "launch" model would not be expected to fit the data. However, neither would it be necessary for support to continuously increase over the 2 years, for engagement to increase, so neither would a "change-to-change" model be expected to fit as well as an "ambient-level" model.

*Trajectories of Control and Engagement.* We tested the "launch" and "change-to-change" models using multiple regression, in which the dependent variable was the linear growth curve coefficient of engagement for each child. Conceptually, there were three kinds of independent variables. Initial level of engagement was entered to control for ceiling effects; part of what determines an individual child's engagement slope is where they began, with children who started higher less likely to increase and children who started lower less likely to decrease. As in other growth curve models, we consistently found a negative relationship between initial level and growth curve scores for engagement.

The second set of variables were "launch" variables, or the initial level of children's capacity and strategy beliefs. The third set were "change-to-change" variables, or the linear growth curve coefficients for strategy and capacity beliefs. In order to examine the unique effects of "launch" and "change-to-change" aspects of control on trajectories of engagement, all variables were entered simultaneously. All four control variables made unique contributions to individual differences in engagement trajectories. The "launch" variables suggested a "rich get richer" pattern in which children who started out with high strategy and capacity beliefs showed more positive linear trends in engagement over the 2 years, whereas those who started with maladaptive beliefs became less engaged over time. In addition, "change-to-change" variables also showed positive effects, with increases in capacity and strategy beliefs accompanied by increases in engagement, and decreases in beliefs accompanied by decreases in engagement over the 2-year period. Additional analyses will examine age differences in these patterns. So far, the connection between control and engagement is homogeneously significant across the age range considered; however, it is likely that some individual beliefs may be differentially important at different ages, especially strategy beliefs, such as powerful others or luck.

## Individual Differences in Developmental Change

The frameworks we are using to analyze the factors that produce individual differences in developmental trajectories can be applied broadly. The time series methodology, because it is based on so many measurement points, is usually helpful in looking at individual differences in intra-individual functioning over short and intense time periods. The growth curve method can be used over longer time periods but reveals correspondingly less about causal processes.

*Intra-Individual Time Series.* The time series methodology would seem especially appropriate for detailed examination of competence system functioning when a particular "window" can be targeted. Because particular life events, such as divorce, birth of a baby, or diagnosis of a serious illness, typically present challenges to the competence system, these may provide a guide for when adaptive or maladaptive system functioning is likely to have long-term consequences. Especially interesting would be to examine differential intra-individual relations as a function of preexisting factors. For example, in our own study, we could use the general measures of control beliefs to distinguish children who have optimal and nonoptimal profiles, and then compare the intra-individual functioning of their competence systems—for example, their interpretations of success and failure episodes (Skinner & Schmitz, 1994).

For normative transitions, such as retirement or the transition to junior high, when assessments can be made prior to stressful experiences, *changes* in competence system functioning could be examined. Analogous to helplessness studies, one might expect no differences between groups with adaptive and maladaptive beliefs to occur until the competence system is highly taxed. In general, the examination of multiple waves of antecedents and consequences has proven useful in charting the functioning of the competence system (e.g., for the reciprocal relations between explanatory style and depression, see Nolen-Hoeksma, Girgus, & Seligman, 1986).

*Growth Curves.* In the area of control, individual differences in many target outcomes can be captured by growth curves. In addition to engagement, any of its components (behavior, emotion, or orientation) could be examined individually. Especially in processes of coping, which take place over extended periods of time, a growth curve methodology could be useful in identifying the factors that differentiate people whose morale, life satisfaction, or emotional adjustment deteriorates versus stays stable or improves over time (Reich & Zautra, 1991).

Some of the antecedents of coping outcomes, such as the severity of the event, are typically assumed to "launch" these trajectories, and this hypothesis can be tested by examining whether growth curves are predicted by initial levels of that factor. Other antecedents, such as personal and social resources, are considered to exert their effects only if they are maintained at a level above threshold. The "ambient-level" model can be used to examine this form of influence. And, finally, some factors, like perceived control, exert their effects more directly in interplay with the target trajectory over time. These factors should show a pattern of relations captured by the "change-to-change" model.

Growth curves also provide a useful methodology for comparing the differential development of multiple trajectories of beliefs within individuals, for example, during adulthood and aging. Change is expected to be more pronounced for beliefs about strategies (e.g., increases in the role of powerful others and chance) than about one's own capacities, and to be greater in some domains (health and intellectual functioning) than others (interpersonal functioning and general) (Gatz & Karel, 1993; see Lachman, 1991, for a review). In addition, because many authors have hypotheses about the biological and social antecedents of these changes (e.g., Gurin & Brim, 1984; Heckhausen & Schulz, in press), the different models could be used to examine them. For example, is a single decrement in memory functioning sufficient to "launch" a decline in perceived control over memory functioning, or does steady deterioration need to be in evidence? Is an ambient level of general control sufficient to maintain a positive trajectory of life satisfaction in the face of domain-specific declines in control? Methods and data are available to test many interesting hypotheses about individual differences in the development of control.

# 10

## How Does Perceived Control Change With Age?

Perceived control appears to be a different construct depending on whether it is viewed from an individual differences or a developmental perspective. From an individual differences perspective, the functioning of perceived control seems invariant. From youngest infancy to oldest age, a sense of control is a source of action and satisfaction, and loss of control leads to distress and helplessness. At every point in the life span, individual differences in people's sense of control are found and they have consequences for physical and mental well-being.

In contrast, even a cursory consideration indicates that perceived control functions very differently for infants, young children, adolescents, adults, and the elderly. At the very least, at different ages, people are concerned with control in different domains and differ widely in the strategies available to them in exerting control and in compensating for its loss. In fact, a developmental analysis of any of the constituent processes of perceiving and interpreting control experiences reveals that they change dramatically with age. Infants don't even develop a "categorical self" to which they can attribute outcomes until 18 months of age (Lewis & Brooks-Gunn, 1979). Children show regular progression in the strategies they use to evaluate covariation

(Shaklee & Mims, 1981). They also change in their use of causal schema, such as the coordination of multiple sufficient causes (Shultz, Butkowsky, Pearce, & Shanfield, 1975). Children do not differentiate competence from task difficulty as causes of performance outcomes until early childhood (Heckhausen, 1984), nor effort from chance until middle childhood (Weisz, 1983), nor effort from ability until late childhood (Nicholls, 1978). Furthermore, children do not begin to make accurate judgments of either competence or contingency until middle childhood. In fact, they systematically overestimate both their competencies and the extent to which outcomes are contingent on responses (Stipek, 1984; Weisz, 1986), a bias that diminishes but does not disappear even into adulthood (Greenwald, 1980; Taylor, 1989). How can the functioning of the competence system be even remotely similar across the many changes in cognitive processing of control-relevant information from infancy to adolescence, to say nothing of changes in actual competencies in all domains?

Initially less noticeable, but upon reflection, equally puzzling, is the notion that the competence system should continue to function similarly, at least in terms of maintaining a sense of control, across the changing landscape of adult development and old age (Brandtstaedter et al., 1993). As life-span theorists point out (Abeles, 1991; Baltes & Baltes, 1990; Brim, 1974; Heckhausen & Schulz, in press), aging itself is a process that in many ways entails progressive loss of objective control. Over time, the likelihood increases of encountering (or watching important others encounter) uncontrollable aversive events, such as disability, death of a loved one, violence, or victimization. Historical changes in the political, social, technological, and economic systems make clear the transience of even currently available options for control. Increasing uncontrollability is guaranteed by the inevitable biological declines that precede death, by the societal restrictions placed on lives by age stratification and stereotypes, and even by the constraints imposed by one's own prior choices. How, then, is it possible for the competence system to show continuity in the face of the increasing "chaos" of typical adult development?

In sketching a framework that can contain developmental invariants, systematic and sometimes stable individual differences, and a large number of age-graded changes in both individual and context, I fall back on the meta-theory of competence as a basic human need. What is invariant across the life span is the need to experience oneself as effective in interactions with the social and physical context. What individuals all come with is that desire and the capacity to feel a sense of control or a sense of helplessness. Beginning at birth, individuals differ in those experiences and out of these differences come systematically "different individuals," cognitively, motivationally, and socially.

What does change are the elements of the competence system and the relations among them. If the elements are considered to be regulative beliefs, actions, outcomes, and interpretative beliefs (see Figure 9.1), then changes can be traced in each. The real challenge to an individual differences perspective is to discover whether and how these normative developmental changes affect the creation or expression of individual differences in perceived control. (For complementary and supplementary developmental accounts, in childhood, see Bandura, 1981; Harter, 1983; Heckhausen, 1982, 1984; Heckhausen & Schulz, in press; Markus & Nurius, 1984; Skinner & Connell, 1986; Weiner, Kun, & Benesh-Weiner, 1980; Weisz, 1983, 1986. In adulthood, see M. Baltes & Baltes, 1986; P. Baltes & Baltes, 1990; Brandtstaedter et al., 1993; Brim, 1974, 1992; Gatz & Karel, 1993; Gurin & Brim, 1984; Heckhausen & Schulz, in press; Krampen, 1987; Lachman & Burach, 1993; Steitz, 1982.)

## Processing of Control-Relevant Information

The research on causal processing in infancy and beyond can be used to call into question people's capacity to accurately process covariation and contingency information (reviewed in Cheng & Novick, 1992). According to a review of the origins of causal processing, infants do not even begin to process causal information before the age of 3 months (White, 1988). Research implies that young children do not utilize all the information needed for accurate estimations of covariation (Shaklee & Mims, 1981), and even adults are prone to systematic biases (e.g., Schustack & Sternberg, 1981). Although the research does not completely converge on the strategies that children and adults *do* use to detect covariation, it does suggest that they typically do *not* use normatively accurate strategies, especially if information is sequential or complex.

This conclusion is surprising to control theorists for two reasons. First, in general, if processing of causal information is so basic to perceiving a structured environment and acting on it effectively, how can people be so bad at it? As pointed out by other theorists (Bullock, 1983; Cheng & Novick, 1992), the interpretation of causal relations is a basic building block of psychological functioning. Second, and specifically, how can children and adults be such poor processors of causal information, when tiny babies have been shown to accurately discriminate and appropriately respond to social and physical contingencies from the first weeks of life (Papousek & Papousek, 1979, 1980; Watson, 1966)?

*Control Versus Covariation.*   A needs theory of competence can aid in explaining the apparent contradictions. First, the kind of causal processing that doesn't appear until 3 months involves *event-event* contingencies (White, 1988). From a control perspective, these are not as interesting or salient to babies (or people in general) as contingencies between one's own *behavior* and events. And, also from a control perspective, the causal question of interest is not, "What is the covariation between my action and this outcome?" (as suggested by the normative standards used in this research) but instead is, "Can I produce this outcome?"

An accurate covariation estimation, which asks whether a cause is a *necessary* condition for an outcome, must include the probability of an outcome given no action (considered a negative disconfirming case) as well as the probability of no outcome given no action (a negative confirming case). In contrast, the answer to "Can I produce this outcome?", which asks whether a cause is a *sufficient* condition for the outcome, uses simplified information, namely, the frequency with which an outcome occurs following an action (positive confirming case) compared to how often an action occurs but no outcome follows (positive disconfirming case). Hypothetically, a baby's experience of whether its cries can elicit attention is not influenced by whether a caregiver pays attention at other times (f [O I no A]) as long as the caregiver comes when it cries (f [O I A]) more often than the caregiver does not come when it cries (f [no O I A]). This pattern of information seems more relevant even to adults (Shaklee & Mims, 1981); it makes intuitive sense that my husband will conclude that he can succeed in getting me to put my dirty clothes in the basket by means of asking, as long as, when he asks me, I put them in more often (f [O I A]) than not (f [no O I A]), no matter how often I put them in without being reminded (f [O I no A]).

According to this analysis, then, the most relevant information for control judgments differs from covariation judgments. Control judgments focus on positive confirming and disconfirming cases. In fact, these are the very strategies young children use in judging covariation, and they are even used by adults (Shaklee & Mims, 1981). It should be noted that children's covariation strategies are considered "biased" (and not simply incorrect) because they deviate systematically in precisely this way from normative standards. In addition, reliance on positive cases for making causal judgments has a specific biasing effect in covariation judgments. When people ignore the baseline occurrence of the outcome, they tend to *overestimate* the covariation of cause and effect (Skinner, 1985a). Or, in the case of young children, they would systematically overestimate the effects of their actions on outcomes. Independent of the study of causal processing, a large literature documents young children's consistent "overestimation" of the contingencies between their responses and outcomes (reviewed in Weisz, 1986).

*Causal Processing.* The more general principle from this research has recently been articulated and empirically examined for processes of natural causal induction in adults. Cheng and Novick (1992) argue that, contrary to investigations of "bias" in causal processing, adults do not use myriad different and contradictory strategies for processing causal information. They use "probabilistic contrasts" or the general contingency rule (Alloy & Abramson, 1979), which is unbiased. However, in specific situations of causal induction, they apply this rule to contrasting "focal sets." For example, the reason that people do not answer the question, "What caused this forest fire?" with "Oxygen," is that they interpret the question to mean "What made the difference between this occasion in the forest on which there was a fire and other occasions in the forest on which there was no fire?" Differences in "biases" for covariation inferences are found to be a function, not of the general principle people use to infer covariation, but of differences in focal sets, either occurring naturally or induced in experiments or by questioning procedures.

This perspective on causal reasoning is consistent with the requirements of a life-span theory of control. From infancy, people operate with the same basic mechanism of causal processing, namely, contingency perception. The focal set relevant to control initially involves the contrast of positive confirming and disconfirming cases. With development, focal sets change, to subsequently include negative disconfirming and sometimes negative confirming cases.

Finally, it is important to remember that, despite the predilection of psychologists for studying it as a basis for causal induction, covariation or even frequent co-occurrence is not a defining feature of causal relations (Bullock, Gelman, & Baillargeon, 1982). The experience of control may happen in a single "action-outcome episode" when one can feel the force of one's actions being exerted into the context and feel the context responding to the actions in that instant. This general causal principle has been termed "generative transmission" (Shultz, Fisher, Pratt, & Rulf, 1986). For tiny infants, these experiences may be captured in interactions with caregivers in which an escalation of crying is immediately responded to with tighter cuddling or more patting; or in which infant eye contact is responded to with vocalizations and greetings. It is also obvious in interactions with physical objects in which the mechanism of transmission of energy or force from cause to effect (e.g., the hand shaking the rattle) can be observed. Because of its immediacy, generative transmission is the most powerful form of control experience across the life span.

## Conceptions of Causes

A great deal has been written about children's changing conceptions of causes. From a control perspective, this work can be organized by its implications for what is required for the self to feel effective in producing desired and preventing undesired outcomes. At each developmental turning point, predictions can be made about the pattern of individual differences in causal interpretations that would result from people who retain a strong sense of their effectiveness as compared to people who doubt their capacity to exert control.

*Infancy.* As pointed out by Heckhausen (1984), extending an analysis of the experience of the self as effective in producing outcomes into "the darkness of early infancy," requires a reconsideration of fundamental changes in both the meaning of *self* and *outcome*. As described previously, neonates have an awareness of and interest in social and physical contingencies, and through this generalized contingency awareness, are able to experience themselves as the originator of contingent effects (Papousek & Papousek, 1979, 1980; Watson, 1966). This initial experience of agency involves intentional exertion of effort, discovery and successive refinement of effective strategies, both failure and success at producing interesting events, and feelings of joy and power in interactions.

The self in earliest infancy that experiences a sense of control is usually considered to be the "existential" self or the self as subject or agent of the action (Harter, 1983). Not until 18 months do children show evidence of a "self-as-object" or "categorical self" (Lewis & Brooks-Gunn, 1979, in Heckhausen, 1984). With it comes the desire for the self to act alone (or as alone as possible) in the production of desired effects. This development is manifest in the "wanting to do it myself" phenomenon, and in children's vehement reactions to adults' attempts to interfere with ongoing action, even with offers of assistance (Geppert & Kuester, 1983; Heckhausen, 1988). From this point, help can interfere with the experience of control.

The emergence of the "categorical self" probably marks the earliest point at which generalized beliefs about personal causes of outcomes can be organized around notions of the self as "good" versus "bad" (Heyman, Dweck, & Cain, 1992). In some sense, this can also be taken as the developmental moment when self and others are differentiated as causal factors. The normative reaction of warding off adult interference is an indicator that children have not only a strong desire, but also a strong belief in their capacity to accomplish tasks alone. Hence, it is an indicator of a healthy sense of developing efficacy.

*Childhood.* Throughout the first year of life, infants "recognize and rejoice" (Heckhausen, 1984) in the process of producing social and physical events, such as rattling, pulling strings, and making noises. Initially, infants' emotional reactions are centered on outcomes and on the feelings of being their originator. Children express joy in accomplishment and rage or frustration when outcomes are not reached. Only toward the middle of the second year do infants begin to regard their creations or products as self-produced outcomes, "to perceive the lasting state of an outcome of one's own activity as an accomplishment" (Heckhausen, 1984, p. 7). At this age, "an initial and global experience of being an originator changes into the experience that feedback provides information about the competence of the self" (Heckhausen, 1984). As markers of this accomplishment, children begin to show self-related affects following success and failure, namely, pride and shame (or embarrassment). Interestingly, as with all subsequent developments, a differentiated reaction to success precedes such a reaction to failure. The salience and focus on success is characteristic of healthy competence systems and supports both optimism and engagement.

The general concept of the self's "personal force," as Heider called it, is slowly differentiated from task difficulty, in a way that task difficulty is recognized first and used as an attribution for failure (Heckhausen, 1982). This may be the developmental point at which "contingency" is distinguished from "competence." At this age (about 4), task difficulty is still self-referenced: Difficulty is based on the tasks that the self cannot perform or cannot succeed at consistently. Again, as in subsequent developments, a differentiated reaction to external causes (in this case, task difficulty) precedes attributions to internal causes. As Piaget (1976, 1978) argues, the successive differentiation of subject and object through interactions leads individuals to first construct an understanding of properties and possibilities of objects that then reflects back on the construction of an understanding of the actions and properties of the subject.

As "personal force" is slowly differentiated from its cognitively egocentric wrapping of wishes, longings, and desires (Stipek, 1984), it takes on the concept of "competence," and competence can be inferred from level of outcome. For the first time, children's competence estimations covary with their performance accomplishments (Stipek, 1984; Weisz, 1986). At this age (approximately 8 years), children can entertain the idea of multiple sufficient causes (Shultz et al., 1975), meaning that from success they can infer that *either* the task was easy or the self was competent and, from failure, that either the self was incompetent or the task hard. Again, individual differences centered around a strong sense of efficacy (which are normative) show "biased" attributional patterns: Success is attributed to the self and failure to task difficulty.

Competence is also slowly distinguished from other aspects of contingency in addition to task difficulty. More specifically, concepts of chance begin to be separated from skill. Children no longer think that chance tasks can be influenced by practice, effort, ability, or age (Weisz, 1983, 1986). Finally, at the end of childhood, effort is differentiated from ability (Nicholls, 1978). Children are capable of seeing ability as an entity that is intra-individually stable, and, with outcomes held constant, shows an inverse and compensatory relation to effort (Nicholls, 1978). At this point, social comparison and reference norms are first used systematically (Heckhausen, 1982; Ruble, Feldman, & Boggiano, 1977). Children can use consensus information to infer both task difficulty and individual ability; they utilize the scheme of multiple necessary causes in explaining extreme outcomes (Shultz et al., 1975). For example, failure on tasks at which many others succeed now implies low ability.

As each causal category is differentiated, children's belief systems about strategies become more elaborated and structured (Skinner, 1990a), and different causal categories and dimensions come to predict action and its regulation (Skinner, 1991a). Initially, a belief in "unknown" causes interferes with engagement; then when chance and skill are differentiated, a belief in the power of others undermines engagement; finally, when ability is differentiated from effort, the belief that ability is a necessary condition for success undercuts action. In some ways, it seems that different theories of control are relevant to different ages (Skinner, 1991a). An analysis of the few studies of age differences in the action-correlates of control constructs supports this conclusion (Chapman & Skinner, 1989; Chapman et al., 1990; Fincham, Hokoda, & Sanders, 1989; Findley & Cooper, 1983; Miller, 1985; Rholes, Blackwell, Jordan, & Walters, 1980; see Skinner, 1991a, for a review).

*Adulthood.* Although less has been systematically studied about the differentiation or addition of causal categories past childhood, a survey of control scales for adulthood reveals the inclusion of several interesting causal categories. The most typical causal factors in adult scales are self, powerful others (such as bosses or doctors), and chance (Lachman, 1986a; Levenson, 1973).

In addition to the three typical causes, researchers have also added "system responsiveness" (Gurin & Brim, 1984) and "powerful others-macro" (J. Heckhausen, 1991, 1993) to tap adults' beliefs about the forces in society that limit and constrain success and failure. In young and middle adulthood, people are likely to begin to experience and recognize the societally imposed limitations on their developmental trajectories. When these limitations are based on noncompetence criteria, such as race, class, and gender, they are experienced as discrimination (Gurin, Gurin, & Morrison, 1978). Other societal constraints are viewed as more general, such as constraints on desired outcomes imposed by tracks previously chosen, or may be considered historical, such as limited opportunities for career advancement in a shrinking economy.

Old age brings with it the recognition that many of life's events are the result of happenstance, luck, chance, fate, or coincidence. Events that are severe, negative, and nonnormative, such as early widowhood, disability, and victimization, are labeled "accidents" and rarely seem to be the result of any discernible systematic influences amenable to human control. At this age, many of the attributes that before were the object of "pride," such as mental ability, physical prowess, beauty, and robust health, are now seen in their decline as ultimately uncontrollable, and as characteristics that although genetic, are distributed based on "luck" as well. Eventually, even societal contingencies, such as high pay for competent work, can be viewed as based on "luck," or at least chance as to the societal moment into which one was born. It is as if, when reflecting on their control as they age, people change from psychologists, to sociologists, to historians, to philosophers.

## Regulatory Beliefs

In contrast to interpretative beliefs, which appear to change in their dimensionality, categories, and functions across development, regulative beliefs (like beliefs about control) seem to undergo fewer dramatic changes. They retain the general shape of their initial form, "Yes, I can do it!" Perhaps the emphasis may shift from *can* to *I* to *do* to *it* over time, as the global sense of agency (*can*) is supplemented by a sense of self (*I*) and grounded in the discovery that action is the means to exert personal force (*do*) and that control may be greater or lesser for different outcomes and domains (*it*). However, the regulative function of the sense of control is a constant across the life span. The sources of experiences and the psychological processes that lead to this sense change with development (e.g., Bandura, 1981), but the power of these convictions is invariant.

## Domains of Control

Across the life span, not just the means of perceiving control change, but so do the ends. Although a relatively underresearched topic, the issue of the development of domains of control, as well as the development of the connection between domain-specific and generalized beliefs, is considered an important, but thorny, problem (Lachman, 1986a; Wigfield, Eccles, MacIver, Reuman, & Midgley, 1991). Do people hold generalized beliefs from which domain-specific expectations are derived? Or do people construct domain-specific beliefs based on specific experiences that are then integrated to form generalized beliefs?

Perhaps the answer to both those questions will turn out to be yes. It seems that young children start out with highly generalized undifferentiated expectations of control that launch their action in a wide variety of domains. Children's differential experiences (based on differential competencies and domain-specific contingencies and interpretations), combined with cognitive developments, allow the formation of domain-specific beliefs in early childhood. The nature and specificity of domains will change with age, however, so that initially good behavior is not distinguished from good performance (Harter & Pike, 1984). Then across childhood, the more normative domains of school, peers, sports (Harter, 1982), and family emerge. In adolescence, when the concept of ability appears, these domain-specific beliefs may be integrated to form a generalized perception of control that becomes a cornerstone of individual identity.

In adulthood, new domains open up, such as work, personal relationships, and civic responsibilities or political action (J. Heckhausen, 1991; Lefcourt, 1983). Among the most important domains in aging seem to be health and intellectual functioning (Lachman, 1991). Compared to children, adults have more opportunity to select the domains of functioning in which to invest their time (Baltes & Baltes, 1990). However, even children differ in the subjective importance they attach to outcomes in different domains (Harter, 1983). In addition, children and adults may have new domains thrust upon them by nonnormative life events (e.g., illness introduces the domain of "health" early). All during the life course, people hold domain-specific beliefs, but the number of domains as well as their weight and personal significance changes with age.

## Action and Action Regulation

Across development, systematic changes occur in the nature of the action repertoires that can be affected by perceived control. The most obvious is the addition of a wide variety of new and effective strategies for producing desired and preventing undesired outcomes.

In this sense, action repertoires become deeper, more varied, and more effective with age. In addition, the nature of action itself changes with age. Actions become less reflexive and more intentional, reflective, self-directed, and flexible. The development of meta-cognitions or executive strategies allows children to deploy their actions intentionally through planning, strategizing, problem-solving, help-seeking, and preventative efforts. A lifelong task is the development of self-regulation, or the capacity to guide, direct, and manage one's own actions. As described in the chapter on coping, this includes the capacity to regulate one's own behavior, emotional reactions, and orientation in service of one's own goals. The development of self-regulation takes on new meaning in adulthood with the regulation of one's own development (Brandtstaedter, 1989).

In exercising control, the targets of action repertoires change as well. Initially, in response to stress, children who do not relinquish control aim their coping at the stressor itself, attempting to change the context or the problem situation (Band & Weisz, 1988; Compas et al., 1991). A subsequent development is the capacity to attempt to intentionally change the self to make it more effective in achieving control—these coping attempts may include learning new strategies or adding and refining competencies. Both these strategies have typically been referred to as "primary control" (Rothbaum, Weisz, & Snyder, 1982).

A later development, only beginning in late childhood and continuing across the life span is the emergence of "secondary control" strategies (Band & Weisz, 1988; Heckhausen & Schulz, in press; Rothbaum et al., 1982) or accommodative strategies (Brandtstaedter & Renner, 1990). These refer to attempts to regulate action in a way that brings the self in line with demands of the existing context. How do people accommodate to decreases in objective control? They select and invest in areas that are manageable, abandon those that are not, lower their levels of aspiration, rearrange priorities, and change timetables (Brim, 1992). They show flexible goal adjustment (Brandtstaedter & Renner, 1990); they select domains that are important and optimize their functioning in those areas by concentrating their resources there (Baltes & Baltes, 1990).

As with all other components of the competence system, the development of action shows differential trajectories. When perceived control is high, action repertoires, based in sustained effortful interactions, are deep and rich; they are organized and deployed effectively; they come increasingly under voluntary control as people discover how to influence not only their own behaviors, but their emotions and thought processes as well. The continued search for satisfying expressions of competence results in many "failures," and these are instrumental in the development of accommodative processes that buffer loss of control and redirect future action to domains in which control is available.

Alternative patterns of action differ from the optimal functioning of the competence system in both degree and kind. As a result of initial competence deficits, low environmental opportunities, or a diminished sense of control, individuals develop impoverished action repertoires. They fail to develop elaborated executive functioning or flexible action regulation, and so experience difficulties managing their own behavior, affect, and outlook. They possess few or maladaptive secondary control strategies.

## The Development of
## the Competence System

In a very general sense, then, the development of control during childhood can be thought of as a progressive realization of the limitations of one's own competence. The infant's global undifferentiated sense of agency is shorn of the power of longings and wishes; bounded by the effects of other people, task difficulty, and chance; and brought up short by comparison to others' performances. In contrast, adulthood can be conceptualized as a time of increasing recognition of the boundaries of "contingency": a realization of the limits of human control and of the narrow range of outcomes that can potentially be influenced by human action. Adults come to know that society imposes strict constraints on the competencies and people who will be rewarded, that history changes contingencies even within our lifetimes, that chance and fate have a hand in all of life's successes and failures, and that the really important outcomes, death of self and loved ones, are out of human control.

The central developmental questions for childhood and adulthood can be juxtaposed. During childhood, how can children maintain a sense of control in the face of the developing realization of the limitations of their own competence? And during adulthood, how can people maintain a sense of control in the face of the developing realization of the chaos of the world? The answers to these questions are complementary. In childhood, children are able to maintain a sense of control only if conceptions of omnipotence are replaced by the pervasive experience of actual competencies, and the discovery of effective interactions with the social and physical world. Children maintain a sense of control by developing action repertoires that give them primary control. If they do not have these experiences, if they do not develop effective primary control strategies, omnipotence is replaced by the development of helplessness.

In addition, children maintain control when they are not caught up in the evaluation of "ability" (or any other attributes of the self) as a fixed uncontrollable entity (Dweck & Leggett, 1988). They maintain control if they are allowed to continue to use personal and task-criterion reference norms, and to use social norms only as diagnostic of task difficulty and not of their own capability. Furthermore, children feel more control when the social context allows them to continue to view ability itself as a conglomerate of "personal force." This aggregate "self-efficacy" combines talents, abilities, and the capacity to mobilize effort and execute strategies; it is seen as dynamic, malleable, and ultimately as potentially controllable itself, open to intentional improvement.

This resilient efficacious self is one of the resources that allows the adult to meet the increasingly chaotic world and continue to maintain a sense of control. Processes key to maintaining control in adulthood are ones that allow people to create and find control, even in aversive circumstances. "Coping" is one label for how people reestablish control that has been challenged or lost, and in so doing discover and create a more competent self. Accommodative processes and secondary control are constructs that encompass ways to divert or minimize the harm that comes from control's loss (Heckhausen &

Schulz, in press). The belief systems that result from successfully utilizing these processes are ones in which important domains are circumscribed within which control is maximized (Baltes & Baltes, 1990); in which people acknowledge the forces of powerful others, society, and chance, but do not doubt the efficacy of the self (Gurin & Brim, 1984); and in which people maintain the optimism that whatever unexpected events may befall them or their loved ones, they can make the best of it.

# PART VI

# Intervention Into the Competence System

# 11

# Is More Control Better?

In interventions designed to optimize control, it seems easy to identify the target outcome: More is better. Voluminous research suggests that both objective and subjective control provide a psychological advantage in most, if not all, domains of functioning. In fact, research on illusions of control suggests that these perceptions are adaptive even when they are counterfactual (Taylor, 1989; Taylor & Brown, 1988). Overly optimistic biases have been linked with happiness and mental health (Greenwald, 1980), and high and unrealistic expectations of control are the norm for young children (Stipek, 1984). In fact, people who form accurate estimations of response-outcome contingencies are more likely to be depressed (Alloy & Abramson, 1979). The implications of such a position for intervention are clear. Whenever possible, people should be given more opportunities to exercise control and should be encouraged to perceive the possibility of control.

Control experts question this conclusion (Averill, 1973; Burger, 1989; Compas et al., 1991; Folkman, 1984; Heckhausen & Schulz, in press; Miller, 1979; Rodin et al., 1980; Weisz, 1983). A recent review of experimental work concludes that there are many people and situations in which increases in perceived control are dispreferred and lead to negative reactions, such as greater distress and impaired performance (Burger, 1989). Research outside the lab also questions the inherent value of high perceived control, particularly in objectively uncontrollable circumstances (Folkman, 1984). Especially in studies of coping with chronic, progressive, or terminal illness, the findings are contradictory (Thompson et al., 1993). Sometimes an *external* locus of control seems to be a psychological advantage (Burish et al., 1984). Sometimes, high internality is associated with mood disturbance; for example, for patients in end-stage renal disease, when disease severity was high and attempts to control the disease had faltered (operationalized as a failed transplant attempt), high internality was associated with more depression than low internality (Christensen, Turner, Smith, Holman, & Gregory, 1991). Christensen et al. suggest that high perceived control can "lead to emotional maladjustment when control beliefs are undermined by irrefutable discordant evidence" (1991, p. 420).

Studies have also begun to directly explore the effects of high perceived control in children dealing with uncontrollable situations, for example, in their families. Can it really be adaptive for children to feel that they can influence whether their parents will reunite after a divorce, that they can stop their parents from fighting, or that they can influence their parents' cancer or alcohol use? Intuitively, these perceptions seem dangerous, and research bears this out (Alpert-Gillis, Pedro-Carroll, & Cowen, 1989; Compas, 1993; El-Sheikh & Cummings, 1992; Rossman & Rosenberg, 1992; Wannon, 1990).

In formulating intervention goals, it is difficult to reconcile the large body of research showing that control is beneficial with the growing number of studies suggesting its disadvantages. Particularly troubling is the research that examines the effects of control for people in extremely stressful circumstances, for example, patients who are in severe phases of illness. Some research shows that high internality is particularly maladaptive at low levels of functioning (Affleck et al., 1987), and some research shows that these are the very people who benefit most from perceiving control (Thompson et al., 1993). In other words, for the populations most in need of interventions, prescriptions about control are diametrically opposed.

*What Is More Control?* I understand the apparent contradictions in the empirical work as reflecting confusion about the nature of control that is psychologically adaptive and about all the elements that are involved in promoting it (Skinner, 1994). Needs theories are explicit about the kind of control that is adaptive: the *experience* of control. This refers to the exercise of means that are effective in producing desired or preventing undesired outcomes. This is the kind of experience White (1959) referred to in his classical article and that has been echoed in more recent formulations (Connell & Wellborn, 1991; Harter, 1978): the experience of being effective, of producing a desired change.

Experiences of control can be confused, on the one hand, with *objective control conditions,* which refer to factors that allow actual opportunities for control (e.g., high contingency), and, on the other hand, with *subjective* (or perceived) control, which refers to beliefs about control (Skinner, 1985a). Objective and subjective control are typically adaptive because they usually lead to more experiences of control. More objective control can increase the amount of control experiences available. More perceived control, by supporting sustained engagement, usually increases experiences of control as well. However, I argue that researchers who find more control to be harmful are examining the effects, not of control experience, but of more objective control or more perceived control. And they are examining them in situations in which higher objective or perceived control lead directly to the *experience* of loss of control. This often results when researchers, in attempting to give people control (or in assessing it in naturally occurring circumstances), omit key elements needed to transform objective or subjective control into control experiences. These points are illustrated with experimental work as well as field research on stress and coping.

## The Negative Effects
## of Increased Control

In order to examine the positive and negative effects of control in the laboratory, psychologists offer people more control and see whether they want it, or experimenters "give" people more control and look at the consequences on affect, engagement, performance, and self-esteem. Reviews of research have concluded that people do not always want more control and that, when they receive it anyway, it can produce distress and impair performance (Averill, 1973; Burger, 1989; Miller, 1979; Rodin, 1980; Thompson, 1981). I argue that the majority of these studies did not actually alter all relevant objective control conditions.

Disjunctions take three main forms. First, psychologists change objective conditions in ways that are supposed to increase control but in fact do not, and in some cases actually have other negative consequences. Second, psychologists successfully alter objective control conditions, but only part of them. The most common situation of this type is to increase response-outcome contingencies without ensuring the presence of corresponding capacities to operate contingencies. Third, researchers have discovered that participants will "relinquish" control to more efficacious others (e.g., to draw blood); it is not clear that this constitutes evidence that people do not prefer control over aversive outcomes; this has also been called *proxy control* (Bandura, 1986) or *secondary control* (Rothbaum et al., 1982)—in common parlance "delegation"—and may be very different from relinquishment of control. Each of these issues is briefly reviewed.

*Objective Control Conditions.* Psychologists have attempted to increase control through many means, such as providing a response that terminates or avoids an aversive event, providing information, choice, or warning signals, allowing subjects to administer their own noxious stimuli, increasing contingencies between responses and outcomes, and increasing responsibility. Although many psychologists, by labeling these manipulations *informational control, predictive control,* or *decisional control,* seem to assume that changing these objective conditions gives people control, this is not always the case.

For example, as pointed out by many theorists, informing people in great detail of the painful sensations they will experience during a medical procedure does not give them "informational control"; in fact, unless they feel that they can do something to ameliorate these sensations, it actually serves to focus their attention on the uncontrollability and aversiveness of the procedure. Likewise, a warning signal long in advance of an uncontrollable painful shock simply serves to lengthen the experience of helplessness. The conditions under which manipulations increase and decrease control are summarized in Table 11.1 (see also Skinner, 1994).

As can be seen, manipulations improve objective control conditions if they change actual contingencies or the resources available to individuals to operate them. Information improves control if it is about how strategies can influence outcomes or how to deploy existing resources effectively. Warning signals and regulated administration increase control if they allow the person to organize responses needed to avoid or terminate the event or allow the individual to brace for the noxious event. Choice improves control if it allows people to select desired outcomes, or if it gives them an option between differential contingencies or differential capacities. Otherwise, manipulations either are irrelevant to control or actually decrease control experiences.

*Increasing Perceived Control.* In a review summarizing the negative effects in the lab that are sometimes found when people are offered increases in perceived control (Burger, 1989), the general point is illustrated by describing "a woman put in charge of an important company project" who has "serious doubts about her ability to do a good job on the project," and in which "the potential advantages of control might be overshadowed by the potential disadvantages," resulting in a negative reaction (p. 247). Burger argues that "when situational or personality variables cause an increase in perceived control to increase concern for self-presentation . . . then the likelihood of negative reactions to increased personal control also increases" (p. 247).

When will "increasing control" result in increased concerns with self-presentation? The key to understanding this argument is found in the definition of perceived control as "the perceived ability to significantly alter events" (Burger, 1989, p. 246). In typical control terminology, this refers to high action-outcome contingencies. And, increasing action-outcome contingencies for people who do not feel they have the requisite self-efficacy, increases responsibility without increasing control (e.g., Bandura, 1977). Burger (1989) himself notes

**TABLE 11.1** An Analysis of the Effects of Strategies Designed to Increase Control

| Strategy to Increase Control | Effects on Control | | | Other Benefits |
| --- | --- | --- | --- | --- |
| | Irrelevant to Control | Less Control | More Control | |
| Information About Medical Procedures | if not related to strategies or capacities | if individual has no corresponding capacities | if individual has capacities; if emphasizes effective external means | predictability; like staff better |
| Information About Sensations | if not related to strategies or capacities | focuses on uncontrollability; focuses on probability of negative outcome | if can brace self for experience | know maximum aversiveness; no catastrophizing about causes of pain |
| Warning Signal | | long before uncontrollable event, focuses on helplessness | if allows organization of escape or avoidance responses; if no escape, allows self to brace for aversive event | predictability; no signal indicates safety |
| Regulated Administration | no perceived control if E will administer anyway; no experienced control if S never avoids event | if responsibility for negative event | if actually do not administer event can brace for event | predictability; no administration indicates safety |
| Choice | if not related to strategies or capacities | if high response-outcome contingency with no capacity; self-blame; responsibility for bad outcome | if between situations of known differential contingencies; if between responses of known differential effectiveness | can promote autonomy |
| Contingency | if not perceived or experienced | if no corresponding capacity; incompetence; self-blame; responsibility | if already have actual and perceived access to effective means | hope for future control; hope to prevent future negative outcomes |

that "the increase in responsibility and concern for a poor performance that accompanies control can also lead to an increase in anxiety.
The extent to which people feel competent to perform well on this
task no doubt influences this reaction" (p. 249). Just as increased
information does not always lead to increased control, neither does
increased responsibility always lead to increased control. Responsibility with no resources translates into the prospect of failure accompanied by self-blame. This produces negative reactions, but they are
not due to increases in perceived control.

*Internal and External Control.* Some reviewers also suggest that
perceived control has detrimental consequences when people expect that a negative outcome is more likely if they exert personal
control than if they relinquish it (Burger, 1989). In a prototypical
study, subjects were offered the choice among administering a blood
sample to themselves (by pricking a finger), having it administered
by the experimenter, or by a confederate volunteer who professed
inexperience. The finding that subjects chose the experimenter over
themselves, and preferred to do it alone over the inexperienced
volunteer, is interpreted as evidence that "people do not always
prefer control over potentially aversive stimuli" (p. 251).

The general finding has also been noted by other control theorists
(e.g., Bandura, 1986; Rothbaum et al., 1982) and is, of course, a common
phenomenon. To explain it, Antonovsky (1979) distinguishes between "being in control over things" (personal control) and "things
being under control" (powerful others acting on one's behalf). As
long as powerful others have legitimate power and act in one's own
self-interest, they will not undermine personal control (Antonovsky,
1979). It seems unlikely that "helplessness" is the proper label for
handing work to a subordinate, or accepting treatment from a well-
respected physician. These have typically been interpreted as part
of the general principle that people prefer to have access to the
means that are most likely to produce desired or prevent undesired
outcomes. In cases in which those means are external to the self,
individuals wish to have access to those external means and they
want the external agents to be responsive to them. People will feel
loss of control if they lose confidence in powerful others or cannot

have access to effective external means; for example, if they are denied access to good medical care.

There is no evidence that perceptions of the effectiveness of others operating on one's behalf necessarily implies relinquishment of personal control. Perceptions about the effectiveness of external means are distinct from internal means (Connell, 1985; Lachman, 1986a; Levenson, 1973; Skinner et al., 1988b). Internal and external means can be forced by situations (such as in the lab) into inverse compensatory relations, such that more external control requires less personal control. However, in real life situations with benevolent external agents, such as doctors or family members, internal and external perceptions of efficacy are usually complementary (each party doing their part) and often are related positively to each other (Thompson et al., 1993; Watson, Greer, Pruyn, & van den Borne, 1990).

## Perceiving Control in
## Uncontrollable Circumstances

The second set of studies exploring the detrimental consequences of control involves individuals who believe they have control over objectively uncontrollable outcomes. Prototypical is the study by Compas (1993) in which female adolescents who believed they could influence the course of their mothers' cancer were shown to suffer from more anxiety, withdrawal, and depression. Likewise, children's beliefs about their control over parental conflict were associated with lower levels of problem behaviors, but also with lower levels of perceived competence (Rossman & Rosenberg, 1992). In the adult literature, adults with an external orientation have sometimes been found to benefit more from interventions (Burish et al., 1984).

In this field research, in which objective control conditions are "manipulated" by the severity of the stressor (e.g., the progression of the disease), researchers have had to rely on assessments of subjective control. In this context, questions about the disadvantages of control might benefit from discussion about definitions of control, including who exerts control and what is the object of control efforts.

*Control Versus Internality.* Just as in the lab, some of the discrepant findings in the field may be explained by the distinction between contingency and control. Studies that show detrimental conse- quences of "high control" usually are based on measures of inter- nality. An internal locus of control refers to the belief that outcomes are generally contingent on one's own efforts or attributes. How- ever, in situations in which bad outcomes are occurring, this contin- gency does not necessarily imply control, but it can imply self-blame. Studies that find negative effects of internality when situations are deteriorating may be detecting the detrimental consequences of self-blame. For example, a failed transplant attempt in the context of high disease severity may cause some people to blame themselves (high internal locus of control), which may produce depression (Christensen et al., 1991). In fact, psychometric analyses have con- sistently indicated a clear distinction between internality for posi- tive versus negative events, leading researchers to suggest that they tap control versus responsibility (e.g., Brewin & Shapiro, 1984; Gregory, 1981).

A direct test of the difference between internality (self-blame) and control can be found in a study contrasting perceptions of "control" over the cause of cancer versus control over its course (Watson et al., 1990). The "control over the cause" items seem to directly tap self-blame (e.g., "It's partly my fault that I became ill" and "My becoming ill was especially due to something about me") and, correspondingly, were correlated with "anxious preoccupation." In contrast, the "con- trol over the course of the disease" items seem to reflect effectiveness (e.g., "I can definitely influence the course of my illness") and were positively related to indices of "fighting spirit."

*Control Versus Responsibility.* Even in studies reporting the psy- chological costs of control, the majority of correlations support its beneficial effects (Affleck et al., 1987). For example, personal control over medical care and treatment has consistent positive effects on mood and psychosocial adjustment (Affleck et al., 1987; Reid, 1984). Likewise, perceptions of control over symptoms and emotional reactions to disease are beneficial, especially when the disease is worse (Affleck et al., 1987; Thompson et al., 1993).

The effects for disease control itself seem contradictory. A careful analysis of items used to tap control beliefs suggests a possible explanation for discrepant findings. When assessed using an item that simply referred to "control" ("How much personal control do you believe you have over the long-term course of your underlying disease, that is, whether it will improve or at least not worsen?"), more control was *negatively* related to mood and adjustment for patients with severe disease (Affleck et al., 1987). In this case, "personal control" over bad outcomes may imply less about feelings of efficaciousness and more about feelings of personal responsibility.

Consistent with this interpretation, when assessments of control included perceptions of *effectiveness*, only beneficial effects have been found. When items mentioned direct positive influence, beliefs were found to have a positive main effect (Watson et al., 1990). Likewise, when items directly tapped the perceived effectiveness of control efforts, beliefs were positively related to psychological adjustment, especially for patients who suffered more disease symptoms (Thompson et al., 1993). In answer to the question, "Is it adaptive for cancer patients to believe that they can influence outcomes in an area when they are getting poor outcomes in that area?" (p. 299), Thompson et al.'s (1993) results suggest that the answer is affirmative.

## Conclusion

From the perspective of a needs theory of competence, the literature suggests both tentative conclusions and additional interesting questions. First, it seems that *experiences* of control have been consistently associated with beneficial emotional and behavioral outcomes. As captured in ratings of effectiveness, influence, and self-efficacy, these experiences have positive effects, even when level of outcome is held constant, and especially when level of outcome is low. Second, blame, either of self or others, is not particularly useful in times of stress. As generated in the lab by assignment of responsibility without corresponding capacities, or as assessed in the field by high internal locus of control in the context of bad outcomes, blame is associated with depression, passivity, and performance impairment.

Third, internal and external sources of control are not necessarily antagonistic. Only on questionnaires or contrived lab situations are people forced to choose between the effectiveness of their powerful others and their own efficacy. The same lessons learned about personal control can be applied to the analysis of "proxy control." If only contingencies between external factors and outcomes are assessed, then high externality leads others to be blamed when outcomes are bad, leading to emotional maladjustment (Christensen et al., 1991). In contrast, alternative "external" beliefs, specifically beliefs in other's *effectiveness* or efficacy, or in their responsiveness to oneself, have uniformly been found to have positive effects.

Finally, people in low control situations have alerted psychologists to the multiple interpretations of beliefs about "control," and the circumstances under which they imply responsibility, self-blame, or efficaciousness. They have also led researchers to reconsider the meaning of both "uncontrollable situations" and "illusions" (Taylor, Helgeson, Reed, & Skokan, 1991). The longer one reflects about these processes, the more one agrees with Thompson et al. (1993) when they observe that "the ways in which people find control in low-control circumstances may be a richer and more interesting component of perceived control than the basic idea that has received the most attention—that a sense of control is beneficial" (p. 302).

# 12

# What Are the Dangers of Intervening Into the Competence System?

A needs theory of competence leads to the simple conclusion that the overarching goal of all interventions into the competence system should be to provide infants, children, adults, and the elderly with opportunities to exercise control, and should also shield them from perceptions and experiences of loss of control. It should be quickly pointed out that the competence system does not benefit from being "protected" from obstacles, resistance, failure, mistakes, ineffective attempts, difficult tasks, challenges, and negative events. Tasks of "just manageable difficulty," which are replete with unsuccessful attempts, are the natural playground for the operation of the competence system, and dealing with them provides learning as well as joy and satisfaction. However, prolonged unpredictability and uncontrollability overwhelm the competence system and, when crystallized as a general sense of incompetence or noncontingency, prevent it from functioning optimally in response to challenges.

Even if one is willing to concede, perhaps temporarily, that "more is better," how can interventions succeed in "giving" people more control or in helping them "take" control? However simple the goal may be, the processes of changing the competence system, especially in uncontrollable circumstances, are complex indeed. How can children take responsibility for their academic successes without blaming themselves for their failures? How can patients rely on doctors without relinquishing their personal control? How can children of divorce maintain a sense of control, so important to continued engagement and optimism, without beating their heads against the proverbial wall? How can the elderly disengage from life goals that are no longer reachable, without falling into the despair of helplessness?

A great deal is being learned about these processes from studying people who deal adaptively with the challenges of illness and aging, and from interventions to optimize individuals' control, which have been attempted from the first year of life (Riksen-Walraven, 1978) to the last years (Okun, Olding, & Cohn, 1990). From this work, it seems that the kinds of interventions that most benefit people depend on the objective control conditions in which they find themselves. Three are considered in this chapter. The first set takes place in situations in which conditions of objective control already exist or can be established; these interventions emphasize changing objective control conditions to optimize functioning of the competence system. The second kind of intervention takes place in circumstances in which control has been threatened or lost and interventions have no power to change objective control conditions; these interventions emphasize supporting the individual in active attempts to reassert control and to ameliorate beliefs that interfere with this process. The third set of interventions takes place in objectively uncontrollable circumstances that cannot be undone or repaired; these interventions emphasize attempts to locate or create control and to actively and intentionally minimize the consequences of unavoidable negative outcomes.

Each of these circumstances requires a different repertoire of intervention tools, but because each is attempting to support the competence system, they also have a set of core principles. The first is that the goal is to facilitate the *experience* of control. The second is that this can require changes in objective or subjective control; and in order to change either of these in ways that promote control experiences, interventionists should consider both strategies (means-ends connections) *and* capacities (the individual's access to means). Third, is the consideration, especially in very demanding situations, of sources of control other than individual responses, most importantly "powerful others," and how these can interfere with or extend personal control.

## When Control Is Available: Setting Up Opportunities for Control

It is most straightforward to facilitate control in controllable circumstances. Interventions to optimize control tend to be focused on institutions like families, schools, the workplace, hospitals, and long-term care facilities, with the assumption that actual opportunities in these contexts exist already or can be established. Nevertheless, even in these situations, interventions can benefit from a careful consideration of how the entire competence system is involved in promoting control experiences.

*Subjective Control.* The most typical attempts to optimize control have involved alterations to people's perceptions, usually through direct persuasion. In other words, children or adults are encouraged to believe that effort is an important cause of outcomes. This is often accomplished by changing interpretative beliefs, for example, by changing attributions of failure from lack of ability to lack of effort (see Foersterling, 1985, for a review of attribution retraining studies). Alternatively, people can be "given" control, by assigning them responsibility or providing them choices.

These interventions work if the only thing preventing people from exercising control is the mistaken belief that outcomes are noncontingent. For example, interventions have succeeded in nursing homes by simply reminding the elderly of existing contingencies (Langer & Rodin, 1976). The notion that interventions to alter beliefs about contingencies can work is also suggested by the effectiveness of programs with the elderly to counter mistaken beliefs that declines in memory performance are inevitable and irreversible aspects of aging (Lachman, 1991).

However, in many situations individuals already perceive contexts as highly contingent; they attribute negative outcomes to their own lack of competence (Bandura, 1977). For example, in schools, even children who are failing do not give up the notion that academic outcomes are contingent on effort; they doubt their capacity to exert effort and their abilities (Skinner et al., 1990). In situations like this, increasing or making salient response-outcome connections by emphasizing the effectiveness of effort only serves to encourage people who are already doing badly to feel incompetent. It also leads people who doubt their own abilities to stop trying, to be distressed, and sometimes to sabotage their own performances (Burger, 1989).

In the academic domain, the problem with these interventions has been captured by the phrase "the double-edged sword of effort" (Covington & Omelich, 1979). Even though adolescents and college students know that they are supposed to try hard and that teachers value effort (the positive side of effort exertion), they also know that too much effort, especially when failure is the result, can be diagnostic of low ability (the negative side of effort). Given the choice between being judged lazy and being judged stupid, most people would prefer being seen as lazy (Covington & Omelich, 1985).

This phenomenon is also apparent with some medical patients who refuse participation in treatment decisions or decline to participate or do not benefit from training on coping techniques. They withdraw, not because they doubt the effectiveness of treatments or strategies, but because they do not believe they are capable of executing them (Arntz & Schmidt, 1989). This is one potential explanation for why "externals" generally do not benefit from such techniques.

For the elderly, this potential scenario is also described by Karuza et al. (1986) in their discussion on helping and control:

> Fostering the myth of self-reliance or putting pressure on elderly individuals to pursue quixotically a solution can, in the worst case, result in essential resources being withheld as unnecessary. Psychologically, perpetuating this illusion of responsibility can lead initially to anger,

loss of self-esteem, and embarrassment for the recipient for failing to effectively solve the problem. In the end, the elderly recipients may feel lonely and guilty for not trying hard enough to solve the problem. (p. 383)

*Objective Conditions.* Improving subjective control only leads to control experiences if people act on beliefs in conditions of objective control, that is, high contingencies and high competence. If actions actually lead to desired outcomes, the competence system then generates confirming control experiences and continues to "intervene" on its own behalf, by contradicting previous beliefs about the impossibility of success.

However, what happens when increased action produces repeated failure? For children failing in school, simply increasing effort does not usually result in more success. Often, there is a serious disjunction between effort and effects. Until individuals possess *effective effort,* increases in action initiation will only serve to increase failure experiences and frustration. Hence, an important step in any intervention is to make sure that objective control conditions are high.

Interventions are usually relatively effective in improving response-outcome contingencies. For example, infants have been provided with control experience when researchers help parents increase their actual contingent responsiveness (Riksen-Walraven, 1978). However, changing individual competence has been much more of a challenge. Changing the repertoire of responses in the individual basically involves teaching strategies or providing resources for producing desired outcomes. For example, in memory research with the elderly, it involves discovering means through which the elderly can compensate for declines in memory performance (Backman, 1989; Lachman, 1991). In medical settings it has included the discovery of techniques for controlling pain and discomfort (Arntz & Schmidt, 1989). In academics, the identification of these more effective strategies has become the target of much interesting research, mostly conducted under the label of meta-cognition (e.g., Borkowski, Carr, Rellinger, & Pressley, 1990; Kurtz & Borkowski, 1984; Schneider, 1985). In effect, adults and children are shown *how* effort can be shaped and directed to produce desired outcomes.

In sum, the most powerful changes in the competence system are accomplished by "performance enactments" (Bandura, 1977) or experiences of control. Setting up objective control conditions and encouraging people to act on them and interpret them as reflecting control seems to be the ideal intervention strategy when control is actually available.

## When Control Is Possible: Regaining Control

Many of the objective control conditions of daily life are out of reach of interventions. Interventionists cannot "fix" the loss of control when workers are fired because of an economic recession; when novice parents are presented with a challenging newborn; or when people are injured or victimized or diagnosed with serious illnesses like diabetes, epilepsy, or heart disease. However, in these circumstances, it can be assumed that control is *potentially* available, that is, that it will be possible for a person to find another job, to be a caring parent to a difficult child, and to regain satisfactory mental and physical functioning despite victimization. Hence, even though interventions do not attempt to alter objective control conditions directly, they do focus on how the perceptions and actions of individuals can help them regain control. One way of characterizing these interventions, as well as the naturally occurring coping of people with high perceived control, is that they support people to intervene on their own behalf to create objective control conditions, mobilize action, and interpret interactions in ways that favor control.

*Objective Control Conditions.* In order to improve objective control conditions, people need to increase contingencies and improve competencies. One good way to discover contingencies is through information seeking. When people are confronted with a medical condition or an atypical infant, one of the most adaptive first steps can be to learn as much as possible about the new situation. This can be accomplished through many channels, including reading and other media, direct consultation with professional experts, and, of course, listening to lay experts or other people dealing with the same issues. Among the valuable functions of support groups are suggestions for new strategies and pathways to goals. Many strategies may sound trivial in psychological terms, for example, the varieties of ways to soothe a jumpy infant (vacuum cleaners, electric fans, car rides), but when these strategies actually work, they do not just produce the intended outcomes (allowing exhausted parents a few hours of uninterrupted sleep), they also inspire hope that the task being attempted is in fact humanly possible. New contingencies can also be discovered that are not connected to one's own behaviors but to the behaviors of others, such as doctors, physical therapists, midwives, and other service professionals. Part of the process of regaining control can be through discovering these new services and accessing them.

Objective control can also be improved by changing the resources of the self. Just like with contingencies, these resources can be both "internal" and "external." Personal resources could include the development of specific competencies, such as testing one's own blood sugar and administering one's own insulin, or learning deep relaxation techniques to relieve migraines. They also refer to higher order meta-cognitive competencies, such as planning, strategizing, and problem-solving (Scholnick & Friedman, 1993); or to allocation of resources, such as concentrating available resources on target areas to regain functioning or compensate for loss (Baltes & Baltes, 1990). The social resources accessed can also be a source of increased control, if they are seen as effective and responsive to the individual (e.g., in the health domain, see Affleck et al., 1987; Christensen et al., 1991; Reid, 1984).

*Subjective Control.* In situations in which active engagement is a key to recovering from setbacks or compensating for loss, a major barrier to overcome is the initial feeling of helplessness that accompanies a traumatic event. Two interesting lines of research suggest that both regulative and interpretative beliefs are important in this process. The first line of research examines the costs and benefits associated with self-blame (Janoff-Bulman, 1979). The simple question posed is whether holding oneself responsible for the occurrence of a traumatic event is maladaptive, because it implies self-blame and guilt, or adaptive, because it implies the ability to prevent the reoccurrence of the terrible event. Research on survivors of rape and serious injuries (e.g., spinal cord damage) suggests that attributing causality to one's own relatively permanent attributes (characterological self-blame) maximizes guilt without providing the possibility of prevention of future incidents, because the causes are uncontrollable. In contrast, attributing causality to one's own responses (behavioral self-blame) seems to provide the possibility of future control without the additional burden of guilt.

One avenue for further study would be to examine whether it is possible to separate self-blame with its implications of recrimination and self-doubt from responsibility with its implications of strength and effectiveness. Research on different facets of internality (e.g., Brewin & Shapiro, 1984) suggest that they can be distinguished empirically. Frameworks of helping and coping (Brickman et al., 1982) propose that distinguishing between responsibility for the problem and responsibility for the solution may be one way to dispel self-blame without eroding engagement in the healing process.

The second line of work attempts to discover how perceived control can be useful in dealing with the inevitable failures, such as rejections of job applications or medications that prove ineffective, that are part of any process of coping with major life events. In interpreting the causes of failure, the critical dimension does not seem to be internality, but rather stability, globality (Abramson et al., 1978), and especially controllability (Dweck, 1991; Dweck & Leggett, 1988). According to this line of work, helpless people use interactions with the environment, especially failure, to diagnose their levels of fixed attributes (such as intrinsic "goodness" or "badness," personality, ability, or genetic make-up) (Dweck, 1991). As a result, even minor setbacks, failures, and criticism are sufficient to shut down the individual's engagement in problem-solving or repair. In repeated interactions with highly difficult tasks, which is characteristic of coping processes, it is clearly maladaptive to interpret each setback as evidence of one's complete incompetence. Likewise, attributions about the task that are stable, global, and uncontrollable also allow failures to demonstrate the utter noncontingency of the task, for example, the impossibility of ever getting any job in the current economic climate, or the impossibility of the baby ever responding to parental soothing. Some of the most interesting research involves tracing the origins of beliefs about the controllability of individual characteristics, or in general, belief systems that hold personality attributes to be fixed, stable, permanent, and immutable as opposed to open to influence through effort, practice, or volition (Dweck & Leggett, 1988).

*Action.* In challenging but controllable situations, active engagement with the stressor is an advantage. People maintain their own engagement by regulating their action, through such means as intentional self-encouragement, boosting determination, and optimism. Action is supported by letting go of self-blame, bolstering feelings of effectiveness, and looking for contingencies. Throughout the long process of job hunting or recovery from a heart attack, these action regulations are maintained by the conviction that there must be a way that leads back to the desired outcome, and that once it can be found, the self will be equal to the task of navigating it.

## When Circumstances Are Uncontrollable: Finding Control

What can interventions to optimize control offer people in uncontrollable circumstances: people dealing with terminal illnesses; the elderly experiencing progressive and chronic deterioration of physical and mental functioning; children whose parents are out of control through divorce, violence, or addiction? One approach has been to assume that, in these circumstances, high control is a disadvantage. The active engagement and persistence characteristic of people with high control could have negative consequences in uncontrollable settings. For example, in studies of children, adolescents, and young adults, when stressors are perceived to be uncontrollable, problem-focused coping is associated with *higher* levels of emotional distress (Compas, 1993).

The "pathology of high expectations" is described by Janoff-Bulman and Brickman (1982):

The most obvious cost of high expectations for success is that they will lead people to waste a great deal of time and energy working on tasks for which no satisfactory solution can be found. People are trapped into doing so not by a history and fear of failure but by a history and drive for success that allow them to maintain a course of action long after someone who had learned to fail would quit. (p. 211)

In support of this line of reasoning, the authors cite studies in which an external locus of control is associated with better personal adjustment to institutions like nursing homes (Felton & Kahana, 1974) and hospitals (Taylor, 1979).

This line of reasoning leads researchers to conclude that the most adaptive beliefs are "realistic control beliefs" (Wannon, 1990; Weisz, 1983) in which beliefs are consistent with objective control conditions. For example, high perceived control may not be helpful to children whose parents have cancer (Compas, 1993) or whose parents are not functioning well (Wannon, 1990). It could lead children to attempt to directly influence their parents' outcomes, and so to experience failure. Especially if children continue to persist in the belief that they *should* be able to conquer their parents' afflictions, they can only conclude that they are somehow at fault, by not trying hard enough or by being incompetent. According to this line of reasoning, illusions of control may be adaptive in controllable circumstances, but in uncontrollable situations, people should recognize their lack of control and give up (Wortman & Brehm, 1975).

*Action Versus Beliefs.* In thinking about these complex issues, I find it helpful to distinguish between (a) adaptive action (behavior, emotion, and orientation) in uncontrollable circumstances and (b) beliefs that support adaptive action. For example, it has been argued that high control is maladaptive because it leads to blind persistence in uncontrollable circumstances (Janoff-Bulman & Brickman, 1982). Although it seems evident that persistence is not always adaptive, it is *not* evident that high control should always lead to persistence. In fact, in the same paper describing the "pathology of high expectations," Janoff-Bulman and Brickman (1982) describe a study in which it is precisely those subjects with high expectations who skip insoluble tasks: "high expectancy subjects are indeed better able to abandon unprofitable tasks when they are led to believe that some tasks may be insoluble"; in contrast "when confronted with a task that they cannot seem to solve, the low expectancy subjects have difficulty deciding whether they are failing because they lack ability or because the task is insoluble" (p. 217). Likewise, the illusion of control, in itself, is adaptive because it leads to positive emotions and optimism. However, if it leads to maladaptive action (e.g., futile behavior that exhausts or endangers a person), then *that* is maladaptive. The question is not whether illusions of control are maladaptive, but whether and when they lead to maladaptive action.

Although a review of adaptive action in the face of adversity is beyond the scope of this chapter (Taylor, 1983, 1989), a few brief thoughts about the issue from the perspective of control are sketched, and then a few more thoughts are added about the kinds of beliefs that support adaptive action in the face of uncontrollability.

*Adaptive Action.*  From a control perspective, adaptive action was summed up more than a century ago by the "serenity prayer." It is adaptive to change the things one can, to accept the things one cannot, and to know the difference between the two. If a more proactive approach is taken, one can also add that it is adaptive to seek the things one can influence and to minimize the effects of the things that one cannot. From this perspective, it is adaptive neither to blindly persevere on uncontrollable paths nor to become helpless. What else is there? Luckily for psychologists studying control, people have been very effective in wending their way through this apparent paradox during times of adaptation to stress.

Recent research on how people successfully manage their own development suggests that helplessness and perseverance are included in the negative poles of two *separate* general dimensions of reactions to adversity (Brandtstaedter & Renner, 1990). These two dimensions are (a) assimilative processes, or transforming developmental circumstances in accordance with personal preferences, which ranges from tenacious goal pursuit to helplessness; and (b) accommodative processes, or adjusting personal preferences to situational constraints, which ranges from flexible goal adjustment to rigid perseveration. Both dimensions, that is, actively attempting to exert control *and* flexibly adjusting to actual circumstances, are related *positively* to life satisfaction and emotional adjustment (Brandtstaedter & Renner, 1990), with accommodative processes or "secondary control" assuming increasing importance as people age (Brandtstaedter & Renner, 1990; Heckhausen & Schulz, in press).

In low control situations, assimilative processes, like problem-solving and persistence, allow a person to discover and exercise control in any part of a situation still open to personal influence. In contrast, accommodative processes, such as lowering levels of aspirations or adjusting timetables, can be thought of as strategies that minimize the experience of loss of control. Minimizing the effects of loss of control, such as by buffering the sense of competence, keeps losses from generalizing to other domains and also maximizes the possibility of future primary control if circumstances change (Heckhausen & Schulz, in press).

*Adaptive Beliefs.* Much is left to learn about the belief systems (or social supports) that underlie adaptive action in the face of uncontrollability. What kinds of belief systems can encourage *both* active problem-focused engagement *and* flexible accommodation? Although many psychological processes are involved in their accomplishment (Brim, 1992; Heckhausen & Schulz, in press; Taylor, 1989), research suggests a few avenues through which control may be useful in this regard.

The first involves the search for important target outcomes that can be controlled. Initially, as in other areas of control research, studies focused on outcome control, for example, in the health domain, on disease cure. Therefore, because (by definition) the causes of stressful problems in uncontrollable situations are hard to control, researchers assumed that opportunities for actual control were few. Fortunately, people in stressful situations have been more clever than psychologists in finding outcomes that are amenable to control. Hence, in addition to targeting the cause, cure, and course of disease, research also now includes perceptions of personal control over *consequences* or *solutions* (Brickman et al., 1982), such as the medical care and treatment one receives, and over disease progression, symptoms, emotional reactions, and effects on personal relationships (Affleck et al., 1987; Thompson et al., 1993).

As research on childbirth and coping with painful medical procedures has shown (Arntz & Schmidt, 1989), even in the context of uncontrollability, training people to cope actively with their own reactions, symptoms, pain, and fear can have many beneficial effects, both psychological and physiological. In general, interventions that increase people's "efficacy of thought control," or their confidence in their ability to regulate their own emotions and thoughts, have been helpful in relieving panic, anxiety, and depression (Bandura, 1989). Naturally occurring self-efficacy for coping responses, or feelings of effectiveness in dealing with the *consequences* of negative life events, appear to have uniformly positive consequences; they are especially critical when the situation is severe (Reich & Zautra, 1991; Thompson et al., 1993).

Does high perceived control interfere with flexible goal adjustment or lead people to overlook other avenues for control? So far, in the few studies examining this issue, it seems that control is uncorrelated with "accommodative processes," predicting neither rigid perseverance nor flexible goal adjustment (Brandtstaedter & Renner, 1990). Control does, however, seem to relate positively to finding many different pathways for control in seemingly uncontrollable circumstances. For example, although answers are only tentative, at least one study shows that high perceived control over the progress of a disease is *positively* related to perceived effective control over other aspects of the illness process, such as symptoms, emotional reactions, medical care, and effects on relationships (Thompson et al., 1993). Thompson et al. conclude that, "those who have lower physical functioning were considerably better off psychologically if they had higher beliefs in their ability to control their emotions and physical symptoms" (1993, p. 303).

Second, perceived control can be helpful in shaping expectations and interpretations of events. In the face of serious adversity, self-blame about the causes is not helpful; for example, beliefs that one's bad attitude caused cancer or one's misbehavior results in parental conflict, are related to feelings of guilt, depression, and responsibility (Watson et al., 1990). Is self-blame the product of high control?

Probably not. A "state-orientation," in which, in distressing circumstances, people begin to ruminate about the causes of events and assign blame for failure, is characteristic of people with *low* control (Kuhl, 1984).

Other techniques for minimizing the effects of loss of control will be discovered by listening to people who are coping effectively with uncontrollable life events. For example, people protect their experiences of control during complex medical treatments by lowering their expectations about specific courses of treatment. This allows them to buffer their general sense that an effective treatment for their condition will be found in the face of failures of specific regimes. Other techniques for "encapsulating" negative experiences in order to prevent them from generalizing across time and situations remain to be discovered.

Finally, perceived control can also be useful in shaping control *experiences* by directing people's focus of attention. For example, at-risk elderly had higher well-being if they felt they were able to cause *positive* things to happen, unrelated to their negative life events (disability or bereavement; Reich & Zautra, 1991). Likewise, people naturally employ strategies to minimize the experience of aversive uncontrollable events—they ignore or "blunt" them (Miller, 1979). When people are trained in its use and provided with a rationale for its effectiveness (Arntz & Schmidt, 1989), this strategy can be an active means of exerting control over their *experience* of uncontrollable events.

In the face of irrefutable evidence of uncontrollability, people can prevent self-blame, guilt, and other damage to the self, by refusing responsibility for the contingencies while remaining firmly convinced of their own competence (Gurin & Brim, 1984). In these situations, individuals decide that they will do their part faithfully and when there is nothing more that they can do, the matter is out of their hands. Often, these contingencies are put into the hands of others acting on one's behalf, such as God or the cosmos, which allows them to be seen as benevolent. Of course, a person can always assert control by refusing medical procedures and treatments whose benefits do not seem to outweigh the costs (Kaplan, 1991), and by the decision to discontinue life itself.

*Children.* Relative to medical procedures and aging, less is known about how to help children cope with uncontrollability in their lives, such as angry parental conflict and neighborhood violence. In general, of course, children should be shielded from these events. They lack developmental prerequisites for coping effectively with loss of control; they do not yet have a robust sense of personal competence nor a repertoire of secondary control processes.

However, in the arena of divorce, for example, current interventions attempt to help children discriminate controllable from uncontrollable aspects of the situation, and to reduce guilt over uncontrollable outcomes and to effectively exert control over controllable ones (Alpert-Gillis et al., 1989). If this line of reasoning were followed in other situations, such as parental conflict, children would be encouraged not to intervene in parental disputes (El-Sheikh & Cummings, 1992). Instead they would be encouraged to reduce guilt by seeing these arguments as "grown-up business" and to exert control over their effects, such as by leaving the scene and going to a safe place (such as a neighbor or nearby family member). The long-term effects of these strategies on the development of primary control is a topic for future research.

## Conclusion

In general, I am willing to argue that it is not adaptive, even in seemingly uncontrollable circumstances, to relinquish control. Instead, I think that high perceived competence and control are useful in helping people to avoid self-blame, to take responsibility for prevention and repair, to find aspects of situations that can be controlled, to act on them intentionally and effectively, and to minimize the detrimental effects of events that cannot be controlled. A tool offered to help understand these processes is the separation of what we know about adaptive actions from what we think we know about their antecedents in belief systems.

**PART VII**

# Empirical Study
# of Perceived Control

# 13

## How Do I Decide Whether to Include Perceived Control in My Research?

The process of deciding to incorporate perceived control into a research project can be long or short. At its shortest, it consists of a researcher asking an assistant to add a questionnaire to the next assessment battery of an ongoing data collection. At its longest, the process can include a careful consideration of the target phenomenon, the nature of perceived control in a specific domain at a particular developmental level, and the profiles of beliefs and the mechanisms by which they may influence (or be influenced by) target phenomena.

The questions with which one interviews oneself in deciding whether to use perceived control are the same as in decisions about other constructs. In the case of perceived control, however, they are complicated by the shadow of success. It is easy to assume that control influences all outcomes in all domains; it is easy to operate on stereotypes about control (e.g., that internality is always better); it is easy to borrow unthinkingly from existing conceptualizations and measures; it is easy to imagine that control functions identically at all developmental periods; it is easy to overlook alternative sources of motivation and action.

We made all these mistakes, and many more, when we started looking at the role of perceived control in children's friendships (Skinner, 1987, 1990b, 1991b). Because of the centrality of peer relations in middle childhood (Hartup, 1983), we thought that a strong relationship between perceived control in the social domain and social adjustment would be easy to detect. And because the emergence of individual differences in perceived control is influenced by early social interactions, and its functioning is so obvious in early family relationships as children learn to tease, argue, persuade, and otherwise influence the behavior of parents and siblings (Dunn, 1988), we thought that the influence of control in friendship relations would be a relatively surface phenomenon. The task was much more difficult than anticipated. Hence, this work will be used to illustrate the decision-making process.

## What Are the Anchors?

The first step is to identify the aspects of the research issue to which one has a commitment, what parts of the problem are fixed. Usually a researcher knows the domain, age group, and target outcome. If any of these are free to vary, then choices can be made that maximize the likelihood that perceived control can be included, such as by selecting as proximal outcomes action and its regulation.

When we specified the framework for our research on friendship, we knew that, parallel to our work in the academic domain, we wanted to examine the peer domain during middle childhood; and that we wanted the target outcome not to be peer popularity or rejection, but instead quality of durable reciprocal close relations with non-sibling age mates (i.e., friends). At the time we began, almost 10 years ago, very little was known about the role of intrapsychic factors, like belief systems, on the quality of children's friendships (for current reviews, see Bukowski & Hoza, 1989; Crick & Dodge, 1994; Hymel & Franke, 1985; Ladd & Crick, 1989; Newcomb, Bukowski, & Pattee, 1993; see also Baldwin, 1992).

## What Are the Mechanisms?

The second step is imagining how perceived control might be connected to the target phenomenon. One basic question is whether control should be an antecedent or consequence (or both) of the target phenomenon. Then intuitions about the process of transmission between constructs can be used to at least sketch a chain of events that links perceived control to the targets.

When thinking about *consequences* of control, it may be helpful to consider the proximal outcomes of behavior, emotion, and orientation, or of motivation and coping more generally, as potential bridges between control and other outcomes. It may also be possible to build a bridge *backwards* from the target outcomes to motivation and action in order to meet control constructs halfway. For example, if peer rejection were the target outcome, it might be necessary to imagine the aspects of social engagement or coping with social stressors that might lead to rejection; the effects of control on rejection would be mediated by these action processes. Finally, it may be worthwhile to think through the general proposition that absence of control can be a sufficient condition for many negative consequences, whereas the presence of control may not be enough to produce positive ones. In other words, the bridges may be more complex for positive (e.g., satisfying friendships) as opposed to negative (e.g., loneliness) target outcomes.

When considering the *antecedents* of control, it may be helpful to consider how factors could influence objective control conditions, the experiences of control, or control perceptions. A bridge between target antecedents and perceived control may be built on such constructs as structure, responsiveness, success experiences, contingency, strategy provision, action encouragement, or translation. For example, in considering peer rejection as an antecedent of control, it may be useful to consider that rejected children experience relatively fewer instances of prosocial behavior followed by positive peer reactions; and, when they do show positive social behaviors, these are responded to differentially by other children, as captured in the term *reputational bias* (Hymel, Bowker, & Woody, 1993). In thinking about antecedents, it will also be important to consider more static communications of control, such as rules, norms, opportunity structures, physical structures, and evaluation and reward systems.

In our own thinking about children's friendships, we decided that we wanted to consider both how perceived control influences the quality of friendships and how children's relations with their friends influence their perceived control (see Figure 13.1). We imagined that motivation and emotion would be the bridge from control to friendship, such that children with higher perceived control would be more likely to initiate and engage in interactions with other children and be more resilient in the face of conflicts and problems with friends. The reciprocal effects of friendship on control would be straightforward: Children who have close connections to other children would see themselves as more competent and effective in peer interactions.

## What Is the Frame?

After imagining the mechanisms, it is possible to construct a frame that will allow the relations to be located empirically. In essence, this means the identification of times, places, or groups of people for whom the connection between control and outcomes is likely to be salient. In general, control is especially close to the surface during transitions, beginnings, novel tasks, challenges, and failures, or in other words, during times of stress. The closer one can come empirically to these situations or groups, the more likely that the effects of control will be overt, especially if one wants to tap on-line cognitions.

Others working in the peer area have also suggested frames for locating the effects of control (and belief systems more generally). For example, Dweck and colleagues emphasize the effects of control beliefs in the face of social stressors such as rejection (Goetz & Dweck, 1980) and interpersonal criticism (Erdley & Dweck, 1993). Dodge and colleagues have examined them in the face of harm done by others and the stress of entering a new peer group (Dodge, Pettit, McClaskey, & Brown, 1986). Little has suggested that the salience of control issues in friendships may be greater for children who have

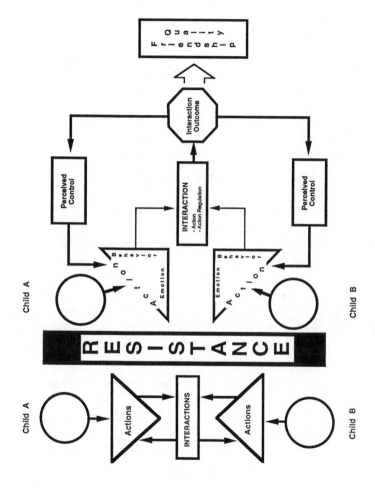

**Figure 13.1.** An Overview of the Competence System in the Domain of Friendship

had to initiate new friendships repeatedly, such as children who move frequently, or children in the military (Little, personal communication, April 1993). In our friendship work, we thought that control would play a special role in the initiation of friendship interactions, in times of conflict with friends, and during separation and potential loss of friendships. We thought it would be less noticeable in the maintenance of friendship relations.

## What Are the Constructs?

The next step is selecting the profiles of beliefs likely to be operative. The most critical aspect of this process is to consider a wide range of beliefs. The difference between beliefs that regulate action (such as performance expectancies, aggregate efficacy expectations, or control beliefs) and beliefs that *interpret* performance (such as attributions, capacity and strategy beliefs) can be helpful in this regard. Regulative beliefs should be important in predicting (a) response initiation; (b) action implementation; (c) intensity of effort and persistence; and (d) performance anxiety. In contrast, interpretative beliefs should be important in predicting (a) differentiated emotions; (b) explaining how prior performance affects (or does not affect) subsequent control expectations; and (c) in linking prior to future performances. Finally, the link between interpretative and regulative beliefs explores why good performances do not always promote good beliefs and behaviors.

In studying children's friendships, we hypothesized that the beliefs explaining the effects of control on behavior in friendships would be regulative ones. Children who believe that they can be effective in social interactions would be more likely to initiate interactions with others, to engage more fully, to repair conflict, and to cope actively with separation and loss of friends. In contrast, the beliefs involved in explaining the effects of friendship on control would be interpretative ones. Children who have more satisfying relationships would take more responsibility for them and feel more socially efficacious.

## What Are the Measures?

It is a surprising amount of work to think about measuring control outside of established domains or age groups. The first issue is the desired and undesired *outcomes* in the new domain. In competence domains, such as academics, sports, and jobs, they are straightforward: level of performance. In the medical domain, less so: health or improvement in health. What are they in other domains, such as family, marriage (Bradbury & Fincham, 1990), friendship (Wheeler & Ladd, 1982), and personal growth? Do the target outcomes change with age? For example, in the peer domain, researchers have identified two very different classes of desired outcomes: relational goals (whether a peer likes you) and instrumental goals (whether a peer does what you want them to) (Crick & Ladd, 1993). When used as target outcomes in attributional scenarios, beliefs about the causes of these two outcomes show distinct patterns of relationships to social maladjustment (Crick & Ladd, 1993).

The second issue is the likely *causes* of outcomes in a domain for a given age group. One alternative is to make direct (or almost direct) translations from well-known to novel domains, such as making social categories parallel to those in the academic domain, including effort, attributes (like attractiveness or ability), and powerful others (like parents). However, it is possible that the causes identified in competence domains, such as effort and ability, may not translate directly to more distal domains. For example, although researchers have attempted to use "internal" and "external" categories in friendship relations, children can also think about "mutual" causes (Ames, Ames, & Garrison, 1977). Or, although stable global internal attributes may be important explanatory dimensions in social situations (Erdley & Dweck, 1993), the causal category corresponding to this in the social domain may not be "ability" but "goodness" (Heyman et al., 1992).

In our own work, we have tried to use an approach that combines strong theory with open-ended empirical methods. We used open-ended interviews in the friendship domain to discover the causal categories children use to explain positive and negative friendship events during middle childhood. Strong theory was used to generate the events; the nature of the probes; and the categorization of causes. Specifically, we asked children to explain same-sex hypothetical children's success and failure in initiation, conflict resolution, and separation with peers. First children were shown pictures and the stories were explained (e.g., "Here's a child alone on the playground on her first day at a new school where she doesn't know anyone. Here she is two weeks later with her friend."). Then, instead of being asked the typical question ("What did she do?") that implies the primacy of *behavioral* causes, children were asked the cause neutral question—"What happened?"—and the follow up "How did it happen that she has no friends in this picture and here she has a friend?". We coded responses by attending to causal dimensions such as internality and controllability but ignoring earlier work on causal categories (e.g., effort, ability).

We learned a lot. First, children's stories were very different than their stories about causes of academic success and failures. In the academic domain, children "knew" what had happened. They were convinced that effort was the primary cause of outcomes, and they were confident of the effectiveness of this cause; they could elaborate suggestions for effortful strategies and had numerous examples of how to implement them. In contrast, children's stories about the evolution of friendships were much more tentative and varied. No single cause was equal to the role of effort in the academic domain, no single attribute emerged with the importance of scholastic ability. Children just weren't sure how these "friendship things" happened, although they were willing to speculate.

Second, children had many more causal theories about the reasons for failure than for success in friendships (see Figure 13.2), older children had more explanations than younger ones across middle childhood (second, fourth, and sixth grade), and everyone could think of more explanations when probed than spontaneously (see Figure 13.3). Third, the categories children did use refused to fall clearly along dimensions of interest. The majority of explanations involved interactions, which are not clearly internal or external, controllable or uncontrollable (Ames et al., 1977). Although actions (of both target child and friend) were often mentioned, effort exertion itself was not. Although some potentially stable and global

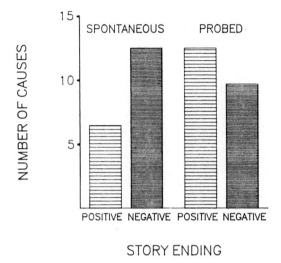

**Figure 13.2.** The Number of Causes Children Described for Success Versus Failure Outcomes in the Friendship Domain

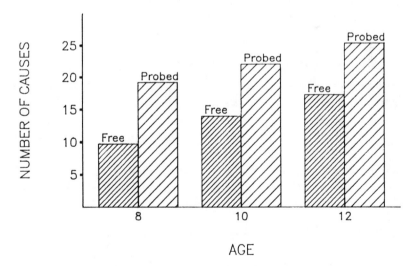

**Figure 13.3.** Age Differences in the Number of Causes Children Described for Outcomes in the Friendship Domain, Spontaneously and Probed

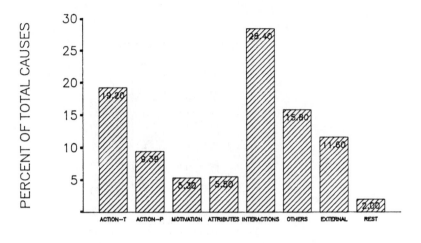

**Figure 13.4.** The Frequency of Different Causes Children Described for Outcomes in the Friendship Domain

NOTE: T = target child, P = partner

attributes were mentioned (e.g., being nice), they were infrequent and varied (see Figure 13.4).

We constructed an assessment of perceived control in the friendship domain based on these open-ended interviews. (Other measures of perceived control in the social domain are also available; see Connell, 1985; Crick & Ladd, 1993; Harter, 1982; J. Heckhausen, 1991; Lefcourt, 1983; Little et al., 1994b; Wheeler & Ladd, 1982). Children found the assessment easy to understand and we were able to chart developmental differences in the perceived importance of the causal categories across middle childhood (see Figure 13.5). They showed the same general developmental pattern of gradual decline and differentiation as in the academic domain, although these changes happened a bit later (Skinner, 1990b).

## What's the Good News and the Bad News?

In any domain, the final issue centers on an analysis of the adaptiveness and maladaptiveness of patterns of control perceptions. In

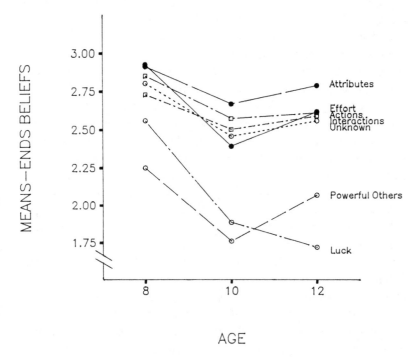

**Figure 13.5.** Age Differences in Strategy (Means-Ends) Beliefs in the Domain of Friendship

general, high regulative beliefs (competence, control, and efficacy) have been found to have positive consequences, in terms of action and performance. In the social domain, findings for regulative beliefs follow this general pattern: high perceived competence and self-efficacy are related to better social adjustment (Crick & Dodge, 1994; Harter, 1983; Kurdek & Krile, 1982; Price & Ladd, 1986; Wheeler & Ladd, 1982).

A more complex question focuses on adaptive and maladaptive patterns of interpretative beliefs. What are the kinds of interpretative beliefs held by people who have strong feelings of competence and efficacy, and what kinds of interpretations of success and failure can contribute to subsequent adaptive action and future perceptions of control? Answering this question requires a consideration of both categories and causal dimensions. Further, these beliefs are likely to change with age and may differ by kind of outcome (e.g., loneliness, social anxiety, or withdrawal).

In the social domain, a clear picture has not yet emerged of the pattern of interpretative beliefs that are adaptive in construing social success and failure. As concluded in a recent review (Crick & Dodge, 1994), "Clearly, the relation between social maladjustment and causal attributions is still uncertain" (p. 84). For example, although as predicted from attributional theory, it has been found that children of low social status attribute social failure to internal causes and social success to external causes, nevertheless, rejected children are the exception: They tend to blame social failures on others (see a review in Crick & Ladd, 1993).

It has even proven difficult to find clear-cut differences in patterns of attributions among children who differ on sociometric status (popular, neglected, or rejected by peers). In a well-designed study (Crick & Ladd, 1993), a distinctive attributional style for popular children was not apparent; and the self-serving attributional bias (internal for success and external for failure) did not appear to be good news, perhaps because in the social domain "external for failure" means blaming others for social problems. In fact, although patterns of relations differed for children of differing social status, indices of social maladjustment were found to be a function of *all* possible attributions for social failure, that is, to internal, external, *and* mutual causes. Even the old standby in the academic domain, effort attributions, seems an unlikely candidate for an adaptive interpretation of social success: Who wants to believe that to get or keep friends, one has to exert a lot of effort?

However, as researchers discover the unique aspects of friendship relations, clearer patterns are emerging. For example, whereas in academic situations, attributions are limited to the causes of outcomes, in social interactions, attributions are often made about the *intent* of social partners, especially in cases of personal harm. Here, it is clear that, in ambiguous situations, benign attributions are more adaptive than hostile ones (see Crick & Dodge, 1994, for a review).

## Conclusion

Although the process of making a decision about whether to use control constructs in one's own research can be lengthy, it can also be worthwhile. It can be fun and instructive to think through the fixed parameters of one's phenomenon, the empirical window, the mechanisms of transmission, the bridges to action and action regulation, and the similarities and differences to functioning in other domains and age groups.

# 14

# What Are the Future Research Issues in Perceived Control?

What is there to look forward to in the research on perceived control? For developmentalists, two frontiers for research on control seem particularly promising. They focus on *mechanisms* and *integration*. Mechanisms reflect the "microscope" of control; on this frontier will be the discovery of explanations, the analysis of the pathways of causal influence that underlie the robust correlations and successful manipulations of control research. In contrast, integration is the "telescope" of work on perceived control; on this frontier will be the search for theories and constructs that define the limits of perceived control. This work will include the synthesis of complementary and synergistic sources of motivation.

## Mechanisms

The most fun will be had in developmental research on the study of the pathways between objective control conditions and experiences of control, and between experiences of control and perceptions of control. Developmental changes in the mechanisms of perceived control are interesting both conceptually and pragmatically (Skinner, 1992). Conceptually, they provide a framework for integrating work from many theoretical perspectives along the axis of age. Pragmatically, information about mechanisms (or at least hypotheses about mechanisms) are essential for interventions. They provide a map identifying when, where, and how to intervene in the competence system: at what ages intervention will be the most effective, which belief systems should be the target of interventions at different ages, and how the social context can itself be shaped in order to optimize modifiable aspects of the competence system.

*Development of the Mechanisms of Perceiving Control.*   One of the most interesting developmental questions focuses on age changes in *how* the competence system operates (Skinner, 1992). Although multiple and changing mechanisms are apparent, their study has received surprisingly little direct attention. Or rather, because researchers have tended to focus on single age groups and single mechanisms, multiple persuasive answers are available and awaiting comparison or integration (Fincham & Cain, 1986). Using the developmental analysis from Chapter 10, these findings can be knit together to form a developmental outline of possible mechanisms of perceiving control. I think that research on the development of mechanisms will reveal that the ways people become helpless and the ways they maintain control are very different at different ages, and that these differences have important implications for the kinds of control experiences that can immunize or disable them, as well as the severity and intractibility of the deficits.

During infancy, activation of the competence system in the face of challenge as well as deactivation when overwhelmed, is probably initially accomplished by neuro-endocrinal mechanisms (Gunnar, 1986). These are almost immediately supported by rudimentary generalized expectations (Papousek & Papousek, 1979, 1980). At the beginning of early childhood, the developmental of symbolic thought opens up the possibility of an additional mechanism, namely, global expectations about the personal power of the categorical self. Sometimes assessed as performance expectations and sometimes as general assessments of "goodness" and "badness" (Erdley & Dweck, 1993), these seem to take the form of summary control statements that are some variation of the prototype belief: "I can do it" or "I can't do it." Devoid of complex inferences, these seem to be relatively situation and task specific, and function to provide anticipatory regulation of action (Crandall & Linn, 1989).

At the end of early childhood, children have available attributions to effort, powerful others or task difficulty, and unknown causes (Connell, 1985; Crandall et al., 1965) and these play a role in both motivation and performance (Heckhausen, 1982, 1984). When systematic problem-solving and hypothesis testing abilities emerge, however, a recently suggested and controversial mechanism may also come into play: mental exhaustion (Kofta & Sedek, 1989; Sedek & Kofta, 1990). This mechanism operates when exposure to noncontingency produces prolonged bouts of problem-solving activity, depleting mental resources. After exhaustion occurs, no mental energy is available to deal with subsequent tasks, even contingent ones.

This mechanism can explain two findings that are not consistent with most theories that hypothesize perceived control as a mediator of noncontingency. First, it explains why exposure to noncontingency leads to *greater* performance decrements than does actual failure, even though failure has a more pronounced negative effect on perceptions of control. With noncontingency, problem-solving activity continues longer, whereas failure deactivates the competence system sooner, and so exhausts it less. Second, it explains why positive noncontingency, in which individuals are told they are succeeding noncontingently but *believe* that they are effectively exerting control, nevertheless produces subsequent performance decrements (Tennen, Drum, Gillen, & Stanton, 1982): Even though people believe they have control, exhaustion undermines subsequent efforts.

All these mechanisms are probably still operating in middle childhood when children's cognitive developments allow them to begin to make inferences about "conceptual" (as opposed to empirical) noncontingency. This paves the way for beliefs in external causes to begin undermining motivation and performance. Then in adolescence, children's developing conceptions of ability allow beliefs in a stable and unchangeable self to play a role in regulating and interpreting performances (Miller, 1985).

In adulthood, beliefs about social and political institutions, and about chance begin to play a role in regulating action. More complex relations among causes can be contemplated, such as additive, compensatory, and interactive (Hoff & Hohner, 1986). Increasingly, adults develop strategies for defending the self from actual and experienced loss of control. A wide array of coping strategies, such as information seeking and goal selection, are developed that allow the self to establish and search for conditions of objective control; coping responses like resource allocation and compensation allow individuals to intentionally increase competence. In addition, repertoires of "secondary control" are elaborated that buffer the self's experience of actual losses of control. In old age, cognitive restructuring through "shucking off responsibilities" and establishing complimentary social comparisons (Brim, 1992) allows objective control to shrink while a sense of personal control remains resilient.

*Individual Differences in Mechanisms.* As each of these mechanisms appear, two kinds of explanations will be required to understand their expression. The first is normative, and specifies why a mechanism is now accessible, that is, explains the developmental conditions that allow a mechanism to operate. Then a second explanation will be needed to describe why a particular individual possessing the necessary developmental conditions utilizes the mechanism adaptively, maladaptively, or not at all. Normative developments may, in some sense, "activate" individual differences in beliefs to begin regulating children's action and interpreting their performances (Chapman & Skinner, 1989).

For example, the differentiation of effort from ability, at about age 9 or 10, provides a new mechanism for becoming helpless (Chapman & Skinner, 1989). Before that accomplishment, children are invulnerable to the kind of helplessness brought on by ability inferences. In tasks in which ability is inferred from failure (e.g., after trying hard on easy tasks), young children do not become any more helpless than in tasks where no ability inferences are made (i.e., failure after trying hard on difficult tasks); in contrast, older children with mature ability conceptions do become more helpless when low ability is inferred (Miller, 1985).

The normative explanations for this phenomenon are twofold. Cognitive advances allow children to understand inverse compensatory relations between effort and ability (Nicholls, 1978). In addition, ability attributions for failure generally produce helplessness, because in this culture ability is viewed as a stable immutable attribute of which each child possesses a fixed capacity; children come to realize this (Nicholls, 1984; Oettingen et al., 1994; Rosenholtz & Simpson, 1984). If cultures conceive of ability as changeable through effort then these conceptions would not appear in children, despite the availability of cognitive prerequisites.

The individual differences explanation also requires two additional steps. For children's differentiated conceptions of effort and ability to affect the competence system, they must have a "style" of interpretations that relies on ability (Chapman & Skinner, 1989). In addition, children differ in the extent to which they view their own ability as an immutable "entity" or as a dynamic "incremental" system capable of virtually unlimited expansion through practice and effort (Dweck & Leggett, 1988). Both a reliance on ability attributions and a belief in ability as an entity are needed for this normative developmental change in the conception of ability to affect the expression of individual differences (Dweck, 1991).

In general, then, future research can focus on both the emergence of new mechanisms and on their differential use. Another interesting candidate for this kind of dual analysis would be social comparison: how it comes to be available normatively during middle childhood, and then how it comes to be used to impede the competence system by focusing on the evaluation of one's ability (Heckhausen, 1982), or how it can be used to bolster confidence and satisfaction by comparing oneself to others less fortunate (age-graded downward comparisons; Heckhausen & Krueger, 1993).

*Mechanisms of Primary and Secondary Control.* Research will continue to uncover the strategies that people use to exert, create, maintain, and experience control. As mentioned in the developmental chapters, for children, studies will concentrate on learning more about how executive and meta-cognitive strategies can improve performance, and how self-regulation allows children to exert voluntary influence over their own behavior, emotion, and orientation. Recent discoveries in the cognitive domain will be supplemented with an analysis of effective strategies in family and social relations.

In adulthood, strategies of primary control will probably be the focus of research on coping, and analyses of the relative advantages and disadvantages of problem-solving, strategizing, information-seeking, planning, and help-seeking. The study of people in extreme stress continues to reveal a great deal about creative strategies for finding and taking control. Research will also help answer critical questions about letting go of control; in the face of potential uncontrollability, when and how do adults begin to adjust interpretations, reset timetables, commit more resources, lower aspiration levels, or even switch goals altogether? Of tremendous importance will be the study of "accommodative processes" (Brandtstaedter et al., 1993): the developmental prerequisites for their emergence in late childhood (Weisz, 1986) and their differential utilization and functionality throughout the life span (Heckhausen & Schulz, in press).

## Beyond the Constructs of Control

As empirical work proceeds on these issues, researchers will constantly be confronted with limitations in the theories and explanatory power of control. No matter how differentiated the conceptualization, or how thoroughly their developmental and individual variations are taken into account, these limitations will remain. A major step forward for our understanding of the self, motivation, coping, action, and action regulation (as well as of control itself) will be accomplished when researchers identify the domains of functioning in which control contributes little or does so only in combination with other sources of motivation.

Ongoing programs of research in other areas have uncovered at least two other sources of motivation and coping. Derived from independent theoretical traditions, they have been studied under the rubrics of self-determination (Deci & Ryan, 1985) and internal working models of attachment figures (Ainsworth, 1989). Along with the need for competence or control, the needs for autonomy and relatedness have been combined into a model of motivation (Connell, 1990; Connell & Wellborn, 1991; Deci & Ryan, 1985). The general idea is that people have a fundamental need for other experiences in addition to effective interactions with the context. These include the experience of being connected to and loved by others (relatedness) and the experience of being the source of one's own choices about action (autonomy).

*Other Sources of Action.* Why is it important to think thoroughly about other constructs? First, sometimes, even when perceived control plays a role, these other issues are equally or more important. Even in the academic domain during childhood, a domain and developmental period in which competence needs are paramount, it is possible to identify other important belief systems and to examine them in interaction with control. Autonomy makes independent and interactive contributions to behavioral engagement and emotion (Deci & Ryan, 1985; Dweck & Elliott, 1983; Patrick et al., 1993); teacher involvement is a more important predictor of children's engagement than the structure teachers provide (Skinner & Belmont, 1993). In interpersonal domains, attachment needs are central to an understanding of motivation and coping (Baldwin, 1992). And during old age, when concerns with competence and achievement seem to give way to an emphasis on relationships and the search for meaning, a focus on control alone would distort the picture of successful aging.

Especially in the study of adjustment to challenges and loss, other needs should figure prominently. Many accommodative processes are not related to control (Brandtstaedter & Renner, 1990); and processes such as flexible goal adjustment seem to require an analysis in terms of autonomy and self-determination. Likewise, important issues, such as when social support extends versus interferes with personal control, seem to require the consideration of the quality of support relationships. Finally, compensation for loss of control would seem to have as one facet, the focus on the satisfaction of other needs, such as relatedness and autonomy.

*Interventions.* For interventions to be effective, they must address the multiple sources of people's needs. And they must provide contexts in which all those needs can be met simultaneously. Interventions that promote control must guard against objective control conditions that have negative consequences for the satisfaction of other needs. For example, in family contexts, it is a dangerous developmental precedent to increase structure by practices that communicate to the child that love and affection are earned contingently rather than given unconditionally, and that children will lose their parent's regard if they do not perform up to a certain level. In a similar vein, contexts that are highly contingent must be sure to supplement structure with opportunities for choice and freedom, if they wish to increase perceptions of control without undermining autonomy or self-determination (Deci, Connell, & Ryan, 1985; Deci & Ryan, 1985; Ryan, 1982).

*Contexts of Human Development.* Intervention studies frame the challenge of understanding why certain contexts promote and others undermine control experiences. A great deal is known *descriptively* about the kinds of parenting, schooling, and medicine that lead people to feel helpless. But less is known about *why* certain parents cannot interpret and respond to infants' signals, or why certain teachers do not gear activities to children's current level of ability, or why doctors have difficulty informing elderly patients in ways that empower them.

In explaining the differential capability of contexts to provide for people's need for competence, theories will probably move away from simple "personality theories" of teacher, parent, or doctor behavior and begin to analyze the social contexts of parenting, teaching, and practicing medicine. In these theories, teachers, parents, and health professionals will be given the status of full psychological beings, with needs and contexts of their own (Altman, 1993; Connell & Wellborn, 1991). Applying some of the constructs of control to the tasks of parents and teachers may be useful, such as determining when certain children produce feelings of helplessness in their caregivers, but a complete understanding will require a consideration of a broader range of influences, including other sources of motivation.

## Conclusion

It is an invigorating time to be studying perceived control. Researchers recognize that control constructs are part of a larger system, shaped by the social context, individual action, and development. A wide range of control constructs is available for study, each with its own strengths and limitations. Work is continuing to uncover new mechanisms in well-researched domains and is also branching into new domains of functioning and new age groups. Theorists are reaching beyond the boundaries of control conceptualizations to integrate constructs from other areas in psychology, such as coping, attachment, autonomy, meta-cognition, and self. Some are even reaching beyond psychology to biology, sociology, and cross-cultural perspectives. The many decades of research and the many theories of control will provide a firm foundation for the decades of discovery to come.

# APPENDIX

# The Student Perceptions of Control Questionnaire: Academic Domain

*Children's Control, Strategy, and Capacity Beliefs (Items and Codes)*

**Control Beliefs**

| | |
|---|---|
| 35. If I decide to learn something hard, I can. | ASCNP01 |
| 50. I can do well in school if I want to. | ASCNP02 |
| 58. I can get good grades in school. | ASCNP03 |
| 10. I can't get good grades, no matter what I do. | ASCNN01 |
| 5. I can't stop myself from doing poorly in school. | ASCNN02 |
| 14. I can't do well in school, even if I want to. | ASCNN03 |

**Strategy Beliefs**

*Effort*

| | |
|---|---|
| 54. For me to do well in school, all I have to do is work hard. | ASSEP01 |
| 22. If I want to do well on my schoolwork, I just need to try hard. | ASSEP02 |
| 25. The best way for me to get good grades is to work hard. | ASSEP03 |

---

SOURCE: Wellborn, Connell, & Skinner, 1988.

39. If I don't do well in school, it's because I didn't work
    hard enough.                                              ASSEN01
43. If I get bad grades, it's because I didn't try hard enough.  ASSEN02
37. If I don't do well on my schoolwork, it's because
    I didn't try hard enough.                                 ASSEN03

### Attributes

46. I have to be smart to get good grades in school.          ASSAP01
15. Getting good grades depends on how smart I am.            ASSAP02
55. If I want to do well in school, I have to be smart.       ASSAP03
33. If I'm not smart, I won't get good grades.                ASSAN01
41. If I'm not already good in a school subject, I won't
    do well at it.                                            ASSAN02
29. If I'm not smart in a school subject, I won't do well at it.  ASSAN03

### Powerful Others

48. To do well in school, I just have to get the teacher
    to like me.                                               ASSOP01
59. The best way for me to get good grades is to get the
    teacher to like me.                                       ASSOP02
51. If I want to get good grades in a subject, I have to get
    along with my teacher.                                    ASSOP03
53. I won't do well in school if my teacher doesn't like me.  ASSON01
38. If my teacher doesn't like me, I won't do well in class.  ASSON02
34. If I get bad grades, it's because I don't get along with
    my teacher.                                               ASSON03

### Luck

20. Getting good grades for me is a matter of luck.           ASSLP01
16. To do well in school, I have to be lucky.                 ASSLP02
32. If I get good grades, it's because I'm lucky.             ASSLP03
49. If I get bad grades, it's because I'm unlucky.            ASSLN01
56. If I don't get good grades in class, it is because
    of bad luck.                                              ASSLN02
1. When I don't do well in a subject, it's because of
    bad luck.                                                 ASSLN03

### Unknown

36. When I do well in school, I usually can't figure
    out why.                                                ASSUP01
44. I don't know what it takes for me to get good grades
    in school.                                              ASSUP02
23. If I get a good grade on a test, I usually don't
    know why.                                               ASSUP03
27. When I do badly in school, I usually can't figure
    out why.                                                ASSUN01
26. I don't know how to keep myself from getting
    bad grades.                                             ASSUN02
40. If I get a bad grade in school, I usually don't understand
    why I got it.                                           ASSUN03

## Capacity Beliefs

### Effort

24. When I'm in class, I can work hard.                     ASYEP01
28. I can work really hard in school.                       ASYEP02
 3. When I'm doing classwork, I can really work hard on it. ASYEP03
57. I can't seem to try very hard in school.               ASYEP01
 6. When I'm in class, I can't seem to work very hard.      ASYEN02
 4. I have trouble working hard in school.                 ASYEN03

### Attributes

12. I think I'm pretty smart in school.                    ASYAP01
19. When it comes to school, I'm pretty smart.             ASYAP02
42. I would say I'm pretty smart in school.                ASYAP03
 2. I don't have the brains to do well at school.          ASYAN01
31. I'm not very smart when it comes to schoolwork.        ASYAN02
52. When it comes to schoolwork, I don't think
    I'm very smart.                                        ASYAN03

### Powerful Others

47. I am able to get my teacher to like me.                ASYOP01
17. I can get my teacher to like me.                       ASYOP02

| | |
|---|---|
| 8. I can get along with my teacher. | ASYOP03 |
| 18. I can't get my teacher to like me. | ASYON01 |
| 21. I don't seem to be able to get my teacher to like me. | ASYON02 |
| 13. I'm just not able to get along with my teacher. | AYSON03 |

### Luck

| | |
|---|---|
| 45. I am lucky in school. | ASYLP01 |
| 7. I'm pretty lucky when it comes to getting grades. | ASYLP02 |
| 11. As far as doing well in school goes, I'm pretty lucky. | ASYLP03 |
| 30. I am unlucky when it comes to schoolwork. | ASYLN01 |
| 9. When it comes to grades, I'm unlucky. | ASYLN02 |
| 60. I am unlucky at my schoolwork. | ASYLN03 |

# Computing Scores for the SPOCQ

## *Full Scale*

| Construct | Variable Label | | Items |
|---|---|---|---|
| **Control Beliefs** | | | |
| positive events | CONp | = | (ASCNP01 + ASCNP02 + ASCNP03)/3 |
| negative events | CONn | = | (ASCNN01 + ASCNN02 + ASCNN03)/3 |
| **total** | CON | = | [CONp + (5 − CONn)]2 |
| **Strategy Beliefs** | | | |
| *Effort* | | | |
| positive events | STeffp | = | (ASSEP01 + ASSEP02 + ASSEP03)/3 |
| negative events | STeffn | = | (ASSEN01 + ASSEN02 + ASSEN03)/3 |
| **total** | STeff | = | (STeffp + STeffn)/2 |
| *Attributes* | | | |
| positive events | STattp | = | (ASSAP01 + ASSAP02 + ASSAP03)/3 |
| negative events | STattn | = | (ASSAN01 + ASSAN02 + ASSAN03)/3 |
| **total** | STatt | = | (STattp + STattn)/2 |
| *Powerful Others* | | | |
| positive events | STothp | = | (ASSOP01 + ASSOP02 + ASSOP03)/3 |
| negative events | STothn | = | (ASSON01 + ASSON02 + ASSON03)/3 |
| **total** | SToth | = | (STothp + STothn)/2 |

*Luck*

| | | |
|---|---|---|
| positive events | STlucp = | (ASSLP01 + ASSLP02 + ASSLP03)/3 |
| negative events | STlucn = | (ASSLN01 + ASSLN02 + ASSLN03)/3 |
| **total** | STluc = | (STlucp + STlucn)/2 |

*Unknown*

| | | |
|---|---|---|
| positive events | STunkp = | (ASSUP01 + ASSUP02 + ASSUP03)/3 |
| negative events | STunkn = | (ASSUN01 + ASSUN02 + ASSUN03)/3 |
| **total** | STunk = | (STunkp + STunkn)/2 |

## Capacity Beliefs

*Effort*

| | | |
|---|---|---|
| positive events | CPeffp = | (ASYEP01 + ASYEP02 + ASYEP03)/3 |
| negative events | CPeffn = | (ASYEN01 + ASYEN02 + ASYEN03)/3 |
| **total** | CPeff = | [CPeffp + (5 − CPeffn)]/2 |

*Attributes*

| | | |
|---|---|---|
| positive events | CPattp = | (ASYAP01 + ASYAP02 + ASYAP03)/3 |
| negative events | CPattn = | (ASYAN01 + ASYAN02 + ASYAN03)/3 |
| **total** | CPatt = | [CPattp + (5 − CPattn)]/2 |

*Powerful Others*

| | | |
|---|---|---|
| positive events | CPothp = | (ASYOP01 + ASYOP02 + ASYOP03)/3 |
| negative events | CPothn = | (ASYON01 + ASYON02 + ASYON03)/3 |
| **total** | CPoth = | [CPothp + (5 − CPothn)]/2 |

*Luck*

| | | |
|---|---|---|
| positive events | CPlucp = | (ASYLP01 + ASYLP02 + ASYLP03)/3 |
| negative events | CPlucn = | (ASYLN01 + ASYLN02 + ASYLN03)/3 |
| **total** | CPluc = | [CPlucp + (5 − CPlucn)]/2 |

## Computing Interaction Scores and Summary Scores

| Construct | Variable Label | Items |
|-----------|----------------|-------|

### Interaction of Strategy and Capacity Beliefs

| | | |
|---|---|---|
| Effort | INTeff = | STeff × CPeff |
| Attributes | INTatt = | (5 − STatt) × CPatt |
| Powerful Others | INToth = | SToth × (5 − CPoth) |
| Luck | INTluc = | STluc × (5 − CPluc) |

### Cumulative Effects on Motivation and Performance

| | | |
|---|---|---|
| Promote | Promote = | (CON × 4) = (STeff × CPeffp) + [(5 − STatt) × CPattp] + (CPothp × 4) + (CPlucp × 4) |
| Undermine | Undermine = | (STunk × 4) + (CPeffn × 4) + (CPattn × 4) + (SToth × CPothn) + (STluc × CPlucn) |
| Maximum Control | Con Max = | Promote − Undermine |

## *Short Form*

| Construct | Variable Label | | Items |
|---|---|---|---|
| Control Beliefs | CON | = | [ASCNP02 + (5 − ASCNN03)]/2; |

**Strategy Beliefs**

| | | | |
|---|---|---|---|
| Effort | STeff | = | [ASSEP03 + (5 − ASSEN03)]/2; |
| Attributes | STatt | = | [ASSAP01 + (5 − ASSAN01)]/2; |
| Powerful Others | SToth | = | [ASSOP01 + (5 − ASSON01)]/2; |
| Luck | STluc | = | [ASSLP02 + (5 − ASSLN02)]/2; |
| Unknown | STunk | = | [ASSUP02 + (5 − ASSUN02)]/2; |

**Computing Summary Score**

| | | | |
|---|---|---|---|
| Promote | Promote | = | (Con × 4) + (STeff × ASYEP02) + [(5 − STatt) × ASYAP01] + (ASYOP02 × 4) + (ASYLP02 × 4); |
| Undermine | Undermine | = | (STunk × 4) + (ASYEN01 × 4) + (ASYAN02 × 4) + (SToth × ASYON02) + (STluc × ASYLN03); |
| Maximum Control | Con Max | = | Promote − Undermine |

# References

Abeles, R. (1991). Sense of control, quality of life, and frail older people. In J. Birrin, J. Lubben, J. Rowe, & D. Deutchman (Eds.), *The concept and measure of quality of life in the frail elderly* (pp. 297-314). San Diego, CA: Academic Press.

Abramson, L. Y., Seligman, M.E.P., & Teasdale, J. D. (1978). Learned helplessness in humans. *Journal of Abnormal Psychology, 87,* 49-74.

Affleck, G., Tennen, H., Pfeiffer, C., & Fifield, J. (1987). Appraisals of control and predictability in adapting to a chronic disease. *Journal of Personality and Social Psychology, 53*(2), 273-279.

Ainsworth, M.D.S. (1967). *Infancy in Uganda: Infant care and growth of love.* Baltimore, MD: Johns Hopkins University Press.

Ainsworth, M.D.S. (1979). Infant-mother attachment. *American Psychologist, 34*(10), 932-937.

Ainsworth, M.D.S. (1989). Attachments beyond infancy. *American Psychologist, 44,* 709-716.

Ainsworth, M.D.S., & Bell, S. M. (1974). Mother-infant interaction and the development of competence. In K. S. Connolly & J. S. Bruner (Eds.), *The growth of competence.* New York: Academic Press.

Alloy, L. B., & Abramson, L. Y. (1979). Judgment of contingency in depressed and nondepressed students: Sadder but wiser? *Journal of Experimental Psychology: General, 18,* 441-485.

Alpert-Gillis, L. J., Pedro-Carroll, J. L., & Cowen, E. L. (1989). The Children of Divorce Intervention Program: Development, implementation, and evaluation of a program for young urban children. *Journal of Consulting and Clinical Psychology, 57,* 583-589.

Altman, J. H. (1993). *How do proximal and distal school contexts influence teacher motivation? A study of the effects of student engagement and school climate on elementary and middle school teachers' motivation in the classroom.* Unpublished doctoral dissertation, Graduate School of Education and Human Development, University of Rochester, Rochester, NY.

Ames, C., & Ames, R. (1984). *Research on motivation in education: Vol. 1. Student motivation.* San Diego, CA: Academic Press.

Ames, C., & Ames, R. (1985). *Research on motivation in education: Vol. 2. The classroom milieu.* San Diego, CA: Academic Press.

Ames, R., Ames, C., & Garrison, W. (1977). Children's causal ascriptions for positive and negative interpersonal outcomes. *Psychological Reports, 41,* 595-602.

Antonovsky, A. (1979). *Health, stress and coping.* San Francisco: Jossey-Bass.

Arntz, A., & Schmidt, A.J.M. (1989). Perceived control and the experience of pain. In A. Steptoe & A. Appels (Eds.), *Stress, personal control and health* (pp. 131-161). Brussels & Luxembourg: John Wiley.

Atkinson, J. W. (1957). Motivational determinants of risk-taking behavior. *Psychological Review, 64,* 359-372.

Averill, J. R. (1973). Personal control over aversive stimuli and its relationship to stress. *Psychological Bulletin, 80*(4), 286-303.

Backman, L. (1989). Varieties of memory compensation by older adults in episodic remembering. In L. W. Poon, D. C. Rubin, & B. A. Wilson (Eds.), *Everyday cognition in adulthood and late life* (pp. 509-544). New York: Cambridge University Press.

Baldwin, M. W. (1992). Relational schemas and the processing of social information. *Psychological Bulletin, 112,* 461-484.

Baltes, M. M., & Baltes, P. B. (1986). *The psychology of control and aging.* Hillsdale, NJ: Lawrence Erlbaum.

Baltes, M. M., & Reisenzein, R. (1986). The social world in long-term care institutions: Psychosocial control toward dependency? In M. M. Baltes & P. B. Baltes (Eds.), *The psychology of control and aging* (pp. 315-343). Hillsdale, NJ: Lawrence Erlbaum.

Baltes, P. B. (1987). Theoretical propositions of life-span developmental psychology: On the dynamics between growth and decline. *Developmental Psychology, 23,* 611-626.

Baltes, P. B., & Baltes, M. M. (1990). Psychological perspectives on successful aging: The model of selective optimization with compensation. In P. B. Baltes & M. M. Baltes (Eds.), *Successful aging: Perspectives from the behavioral sciences* (pp. 1-34). Cambridge, UK: Cambridge University Press.

Baltes, P. B., Reese, H. W., & Nesselroade, J. R. (1977). *Life-span developmental psychology: Introduction to research methods.* Monterey, CA: Brooks/Cole.

Band, E., & Weisz, J. R. (1988). How to feel better when it feels bad: Children's perspectives on coping with everyday stress. *Developmental Psychology, 24,* 247-253.

Bandura, A. (1977). Self-efficacy: Toward a unified theory of behavioral change. *Psychological Review, 84,* 191-215.

Bandura, A. (1981). Self-referent thought: A developmental analysis of self-efficacy. In J. H. Flavell & L. Ross (Eds.), *Social cognitive development: Frontiers and possible futures* (pp. 200-239). Cambridge, UK: Cambridge University Press.

Bandura, A. (1986). *The social foundations of thought and action: A social cognitive theory.* Englewood Cliffs, NJ: Prentice Hall.

Bandura, A. (1989). Human agency in social cognitive theory. *American Psychologist, 44*(9), 1175-1184.

Bandura, A., & Schunk, D. H. (1981). Cultivating competence, self-efficacy, and intrinsic interest through proximal self-motivation. *Journal of Personality and Social Psychology, 41*, 586-598.

Barker, G. P., & Graham, S. (1987). Developmental study of praise and blame as attributional cues. *Journal of Educational Psychology, 79*, 62-66.

Baumrind, D. (1977, March). *Socialization determinants of personal agency.* Paper presented at the Biennial Meeting of the Society for Research in Child Development, New Orleans.

Belmont, M., Skinner, E., Wellborn, J., & Connell, J. (1988). *Teacher as social context: A measure of student perceptions of teacher provision of involvement, structure, and autonomy support.* Technical report, University of Rochester, New York.

Berry, J. M., & West, R. L. (1993). Cognitive self-efficacy in relation to personal mastery and goal setting across the life span. *International Journal of Behavioral Development, 16*(2), 351-379.

Boesch, E. E. (1976). *Psychopathologie des alltags* [Everyday psychopathology]. Bern, Switzerland: Huber.

Burkowski, J. G., Carr, M., Rellinger, E., & Pressley, M. (1990). Self-regulated cognition: Interdependence of metacognition, attributions, and self-esteem. In B. Jones & L. Idol (Eds.), *Dimensions of thinking* (pp. 53-92). Hillsdale, NJ: Lawrence Erlbaum.

Bowlby, J. (1969). *Attachment and loss: Vol. 1. Attachment.* New York: Basic Books.

Bradbury, T. N., & Fincham, F. D. (1990). Attributions in marriage: Review and critique. *Psychological Bulletin, 107*(1), 3-33.

Brandtstaedter, J. (1989). Personal self-regulation of development: Cross-sequential analyses of development-related control beliefs and emotions. *Developmental Psychology, 25*, 96-108.

Brandtstaedter, J., & Renner, G. (1990). Tenacious goal pursuit and flexible goal adjustment: Explication and age-related analysis of assimilative and accommodative strategies of coping. *Psychology and Aging, 5*(1), 58-67.

Brandtstaedter, J., Krampen, G., & Heil, F. E. (1986). Personal control and emotional evaluation of development in partnership relations during adulthood. In M. M. Baltes & P. B. Baltes (Eds.), *The psychology of control and aging* (pp. 265-296). Hillsdale, NJ: Lawrence Erlbaum.

Brandtstaedter, J., Wentura, D., & Greve, W. (1993). Adaptive resources of the aging self: Outlines of an emergent perspective. *International Journal of Behavioral Development, 16*(2), 323-349.

Brewin, C. R., & Shapiro, D. A. (1984). Beyond locus of control: Attribution of responsibility for positive and negative outcomes. *British Journal of Psychology, 75*, 43-49.

Brickman, P., Rabinowitz, V. C., Karuza, J., Jr., Coates, D., Cohn, E., & Kidder, L. (1982). Models of helping and coping. *American Psychologist, 37*, 368-384.

Brim, O. G., Jr. (1974, September). *The sense of personal control over one's life.* Invited address at the 82nd Annual Convention of the American Psychological Association, New Orleans.

Brim, O. G., Jr. (1976). Life span development of the theory of oneself: Implications for child development. In H. W. Reese (Ed.), *Advances in child development and behavior* (Vol. 11). New York: Academic Press.

Brim, O. G. (1992). *Ambition: How we manage success and failure throughout our lives.* New York: Basic Books.

Bukowski, W. M., & Hoza, B. (1989). Popularity and friendship: Issues in theory, measurement, and outcome. In T. Berndt & G. Ladd (Eds.), *Peer relationships in child development* (pp. 15-45). New York: John Wiley.

Bullock, M. (1983, April). *Causal reasoning and developmental change over the preschool years.* Paper presented at the biennial meetings of the Society for Research in Child Development, Vancouver, British Columbia.

Bullock, M., Gelman, R., & Baillargeon, R. (1982). The development of causal reasoning. In W. Friedman (Ed.), *The developmental psychology of time* (pp. 209-254). New York: Academic Press.

Burger, J. M. (1989). Negative reactions to increases in perceived personal control. *Journal of Personality and Social Psychology, 56*(2), 246-256.

Burish, T. G., Carey, M. P., Wallston, K. A., Stein, M. J., Jamison, R. N., & Lyles, J. N. (1984). Health locus of control and chronic disease: An external orientation may be advantageous. *Journal of Social and Clinical Psychology, 2*(4), 326-332.

Chapman, M., & Skinner, E. A. (1985). Action in development/Development in action. In M. Frese & J. Sabini (Eds.), *Goal directed behavior: The concept of action in psychology* (pp. 199-213). Hillsdale, NJ: Lawrence Erlbaum.

Chapman, M., & Skinner, E. A. (1989). Children's agency beliefs, cognitive performance and conceptions of effort and ability: Interaction of individual and developmental differences. *Child Development, 60,* 1229-1238.

Chapman, M., Skinner, E. A., & Baltes, P. B. (1990). Interpreting correlations between children's perceived control and cognitive performance: Control, agency, or means-ends beliefs? *Developmental Psychology, 26,* 244-251.

Cheng, P. W., & Novick, L. R. (1992). Covariation in natural causal induction. *Psychological Review, 99*(2), 365-382.

Christensen, A. J., Turner, C. W., Smith, T. W., Holman, J. M., & Gregory, M. C. (1991). Health locus of control and depression in end-stage renal disease. *Journal of Consulting and Clinical Psychology, 59*(3), 419-424.

Cofer, C. N. (1985). Drives and motives. In G. A. Kimble & K. Schlesinger (Eds.), *Topics in the history of psychology* (pp. 151-190). Hillsdale, NJ: Lawrence Erlbaum.

Compas, B. E. (1993, April). *An analysis of "good" stress and coping in adolescence.* In E. Skinner (Chair). *The search for "good" stress and coping: An analysis of developmentally adaptive stress across the life span.* Symposium presented at the 60th meeting of the Society for Research in Child Development, New Orleans.

Compas, B. E. (1987). Coping with stress during childhood and adolescence. *Psychological Bulletin, 101,* 393-403.

Compas, B. E., Banez, G. A., Malcarne, V., & Worsham, N. (1991). Perceived control and coping with stress: A developmental perspective. *Journal of Social Issues, 47*(4), 23-34.

Compas, B. E., & Worsham, N. (1991, April). *When mom or dad has cancer: Developmental differences in children's coping with family stress.* Paper presented at the meetings of the Society for Research on Child Development, Seattle.

Connell, J. P. (1985). A new multidimensional measure of children's perceptions of control. *Child Development, 56,* 1011-1018.

Connell, J. P. (1990). Context, self and action: A motivational analysis of self-esteem processes across the life-span. In D. Cicchetti & M. Beeghly (Eds.), *The self in transition: From infancy to childhood* (pp. 61-97). Chicago: University of Chicago Press.

Connell, J. P., & Furman, W. (1984). Conceptual and methodological considerations in the study of transition. In R. Emde & R. Harmon (Eds.), *Continuities and discontinuities in development* (pp. 153-173). New York: Plenum.

Connell, J. P., & Skinner, E. A. (1990, April). Predicting trajectories of academic engagement: A growth curve analysis of children's motivation in school. In P. Wood (Chair), *Methodological advances in the study of change processes in education.* Symposium presented at the meetings of the American Educational Research Association, Boston.

Connell, J. P., & Wellborn, J. G. (1991). Competence, autonomy and relatedness: A motivational analysis of self-system processes. In M. Gunnar & A. Sroufe (Eds.), *Minnesota Symposium on Child Psychology* (pp. 43-77). Chicago: University of Chicago Press.

Covington, M. V., & Omelich, C. L. (1979). Effort: The double-edged sword in school achievement. *Journal of Educational Psychology, 71,* 169-182.

Covington, M. V., & Omelich, C. L. (1985). Ability and effort valuation among failure-avoiding and failure-accepting students. *Journal of Educational Psychology, 77,* 446-459.

Crandall, V. C., & Battle, E. S. (1970). Antecedents and adult correlates of academic and intellectual achievement effort. *Minnesota Symposia on Child Psychology, 4,* 39-93.

Crandall, V. C., & Crandall, B. W. (1983). Maternal and childhood behaviors as antecedents of internal-external control perceptions in young adulthood. In H. M. Lefcourt (Ed.), *Research with the locus of control construct: Vol. 2. Developments and social problems* (pp. 53-103). New York: Academic Press.

Crandall, V. C., & Linn, P. L. (1989, April). Children's achievement orientation: Sex differences, developmental trends, and emergence of motivational functions. In J. G. Nicholls (Chair), *Achievement strivings, expectations, and values in the toddler to first grade years.* Symposium presented at the Meetings of the Society for Research in Child Development, Kansas City.

Crandall, V. C., Katkovsky, W., & Crandall, V. J. (1965). Children's beliefs in their control of reinforcement in intellectual academic achievement behaviors. *Child Development, 36,* 91-109.

Crandall, V. J. (1973). *Differences in parental antecedents of internal-external control in children and in young adulthood.* Paper presented at the Meetings of the American Psychological Association, Montreal.

Crick, N. R., & Dodge, K. A. (1994). A review and reformulation of social information-processing mechanisms in children's social adjustment. *Psychological Bulletin, 115*(1), 74-101.

Crick, N. R., & Ladd, G. W. (1990). Children's perspectives of the outcomes of social strategies: Do the ends justify being mean? *Developmental Psychology, 26,* 612-620.

Crick, N. R., & Ladd, G. W. (1993). Children's perceptions of their peer experiences: Attributions, loneliness, social anxiety, and social avoidance. *Developmental Psychology, 29*(2), 244-254.

Crittendon, P. M. (1990). Internal representational models of attachment relationships. *Infant Mental Health Journal, 11,* 259-277.

DeCharms, R. (1968). *Personal causation.* New York: Academic Press.

DeCharms, R. (1981). Personal causation and locus of control: Two different traditions and two uncorrelated constructs. In H. M. Lefcourt (Ed.), *Research with the locus of control construct: Vol. 1. Assessments and methods* (pp. 337-358). San Diego, CA: Academic Press.

Deci, E. L. (1975). *Intrinsic motivation.* New York: Plenum.

Deci, E. L. (1992). The history of motivation in psychology and its relevance for management. In V. H. Vroom & E. L. Deci (Eds.), *Management and motivation* (2nd ed.; pp. 9-29). London: Penguin.

Deci, E. L., Connell, J. P., & Ryan, R. M. (1985). A motivational analysis of self-determination and self-regulation in the classroom. In C. Ames & R. Ames (Eds.), *Research on motivation in education: Vol. 2. The classroom milieu* (pp. 13-52). San Diego, CA: Academic Press.

Deci, E. L., & Ryan, R. M. (1985). *Intrinsic motivation and self-determination in human behavior.* New York: Plenum.

DeFries, J. C., Plomin, R., & Fulker, D. W. (1994). *Nature and nurture during middle childhood.* Oxford: Blackwell.

Diener, C. I., & Dweck, C. S. (1978). An analysis of learned helplessness: Continuous changes in performance, strategy, and achievement cognitions following failure. *Journal of Personality and Social Psychology, 36,* 451-462.

Dodge, K. A., Pettit, G. S., McClaskey, C. L., & Brown, M. M. (1986). Social competence in children. *Monographs of the Society for Research in Child Development, 51*(2, Serial No. 213).

Duncan, J., & Morgan, N. (1980). The incidence and some consequences of major life events. In G. J. Duncan & J. N. Morgan (Eds.), *Five thousand American families—Patterns of economic progress.* Ann Arbor, MI: Institute for Social Research.

Dunn, J. (1988). *The beginnings of social understanding.* Cambridge, MA: Harvard University Press.

Dweck, C., & Goetz, T. (1978). Attributions and learned helplessness. In J. Harvey, W. Ickes, & R. Kidd (Eds.), *New direction in attribution research* (pp. 157-179). Hillsdale, NJ: Lawrence Erlbaum.

Dweck, C. S. (1991). Self-theories and goals: Their role in motivation, personality and development. In R. A. Dienstbier (Ed.), *Nebraska Symposium on Motivation, 1990.* Lincoln: University of Nebraska Press.

Dweck, C. S., Davidson, W., Nelson, S., & Enna, B. (1978). Sex differences in learned helplessness: (II) The contingencies of evaluative feedback in the classroom and (III) An experimental analysis. *Developmental Psychology, 14,* 268-776.

Dweck, C. S., & Elliott, E. S. (1983). Achievement motivation. In P. H. Mussen (Series Ed.) & E. M. Hetherington (Vol. Ed.), *Handbook of child psychology: Vol. 4. Socialization, personality, and social development* (pp. 643-691). New York: John Wiley.

Dweck, C. S., & Leggett, E. L. (1988). A social-cognitive approach to motivation and personality. *Psychological Review, 95,* 256-273.

Eisenberg, N., Fabes, R. A., & Guthrie, I. (in press). Coping with stress: The roles of regulation and development. In J. N. Sandler & S. A. Wolchik (Eds.), *Handbook of children's coping with common stressors: Linking theory, research, and intervention.* New York: Plenum.

El-Sheikh, M., & Cummings, E. M. (1992). Availability of control and preschoolers' responses to interadult anger. *International Journal of Behavioral Development, 15*(2), 207-226.

Erdley, C. A., & Dweck, C. S. (1993). Children's implicit personality theories as predictors of their social adjustments. *Child Development, 64,* 863-878.

Felton, B., & Kahana, E. (1974). Adjustment and situationally bound locus of control among institutionalized aged. *Journal of Gerontology, 29,* 295-301.

Fincham, F., Hodoka, A., & Sanders, R. J. (1989). Learned helplessness, test anxiety, and academic achievement: A longitudinal analysis. *Child Development, 60,* 138-145.

Fincham, F. D., & Cain, K. M. (1986). Learned helplessness in humans: A developmental analysis. *Developmental Review, 6*(4), 301-333.

Findley, M. J., & Cooper, H. M. (1983). Locus of control and academic achievement: A literature review. *Journal of Personality and Social Psychology, 44*(2), 419-427.

Finkelstein, N. W., & Ramey, C. T. (1977). Learning to control the environment in infancy. *Child Psychology, 48,* 806-819.

Foersterling, F. (1985). Attributional retraining: A review. *Psychological Bulletin, 98,* 495-512.

Folkman, S. (1984). Personal control and stress and coping processes: A theoretical analysis. *Journal of Personality and Social Psychology, 46*(4), 839-852.

Folkman, S., & Lazarus, R. S. (1985). If it changes it must be a process: Study of emotion and coping during three stages of a college examination. *Journal of Personality and Social Psychology, 48,* 150-170.

Frese, M., & Sabini, J. (Eds.). (1985). *Goal-directed behavior: The concept of action in psychology.* Hillsdale, NJ: Lawrence Erlbaum.

Garmezy, N. (1983). Stressors of childhood. In N. Garmezy & M. Rutter (Eds.), *Stress, coping and development in children* (pp. 43-84). New York: McGraw-Hill.

Garmezy, N., & Rutter, M. (Eds.). (1983). *Stress, coping and development in children.* New York: McGraw-Hill.

Gatz, M., & Karel, M. J. (1993). Individual change in perceived control over 20 years. *International Journal of Behavioral Development, 16*(2), 305-322.

Geppert, U., & Kuester, U. (1983). The emergence of "wanting to do it oneself": A precursor of achievement motivation. *International Journal of Behavioral Development, 6,* 355-369.

Goetz, T. W., & Dweck, C. S. (1980). Learned helplessness in social situations. *Journal of Personality and Social Psychology, 39,* 246-255.

Goldstein, R. (1983). *The mind-body problem.* New York: Random House.

Graham, S. (1984). Communicating sympathy and anger to black and white children: The cognitive (attributional) consequences of affective cues. *Journal of Personality and Social Psychology, 47,* 40-54.

Greenwald, A. G. (1980). The totalitarian ego: Fabrication and revision of personal history. *American Psychologist, 35,* 603-618.

Gregory, W. L. (1981). Expectancies for controllability, performance attributions, and behavior. In H. M. Lefcourt (Ed.), *Research with the locus of control construct* (Vol. 1, pp. 67-124). New York: Academic Press.

Grolnick, W., & Bridges, L. (1993, April). *An analysis of "good" stress and coping in infancy and toddlerhood.* In E. Skinner (Chair). *The search for "good" stress and coping: An analysis of developmentally adaptive stress across the life span.* Symposium presented at the 60th meeting of the Society for Research in Child Development, New Orleans.

Grolnick, W. S., & Ryan, R. M. (1989). Parent styles associated with children's self-regulation and competence: A social contextual perspective. *Journal of Educational Psychology, 81,* 143-154.

Gunnar, M. R. (1980). Contingent stimulation: A review of its role in early development. In S. Levine & H. Ursin (Eds.), *Coping and health* (pp. 101-119). New York: Plenum.

Gunnar, M. R. (1986). Human developmental psychoneuroendocrinology: A review of research on neuroendocrine responses to challenge and threat in infancy and childhood. In M. E. Lamb, A. L. Brun, & B. Nopeff (Eds.), *Advances in developmental psychology* (pp. 51-103). Hillsdale, NJ: Lawrence Erlbaum.

Gunnar, M. R. (1989). Studies of the human infant's adrenocortical response to potentially stressful events. *New Directions for Child Development, 45*(Fall), 3-18.

Gurin, P., & Brim, O. G. (1984). Change in self in adulthood: The example of sense of control. In P. B. Baltes & O. G. Brim (Eds.), *Life-span development and behavior* (pp. 282-334). New York: Academic Press.

Gurin, P., Gurin, G., & Morrison, B. M. (1978). Personal and ideological aspects of internal-external control. *Social Psychology, 41,* 275-296.

Harter, S. (1978). Effectance motivation reconsidered: Toward a developmental model. *Human Development, 21,* 36-64.

Harter, S. (1982). The perceived competence scale for children. *Child Development, 53,* 89-97.

Harter, S. (1983). Developmental perspectives on the self system. In E. M. Hetherington (Ed.), *Handbook of child psychology: Vol. 4. Socialization, personality, and social development* (pp. 275-385). New York: John Wiley.

Harter, S., & Pike, R. (1984). The pictorial scale of perceived competence and social competence for young children. *Child Development, 55,* 1969-1982.

Hartup, W. W. (1983). Peer relations. In E. M. Hetherington (Ed.), *Handbook of child psychology: Vol. 4. Socialization, personality, and social development* (pp. 103-198). New York: John Wiley.

Heckhausen, H. (1977). Achievement motivation and its constructs: A cognitive model. *Motivation and Emotion, 1,* 283-329.

Heckhausen, H. (1982). The development of achievement motivation. In W. W. Hartup (Ed.), *Review of child development research* (Vol. 6, pp. 600-668). Chicago: University of Chicago Press.

Heckhausen, H. (1984). Emergent achievement behavior: Some early developments. In M. Haehr (Ed.), *Advances in motivation and achievement* (pp. 1-32). Greenwich, CT: JAI Press.

Heckhausen, H. (1991). *Motivation and action.* Berlin: Springer-Verlag.

Heckhausen, H., & Gollwitzer, P. M. (1987). Thought contents and cognitive functioning in motivational versus volitional states of mind. *Motivation and Emotion, 11*(2), 101-120.

Heckhausen, J. (1988). Becoming aware of one's competence in the second year: Developmental progression within the mother-child dyad. *International Journal of Behavioral Development, 11*, 305-326.

Heckhausen, J. (1991). *CASE-A, Causality and Self-Efficacy in Adulthood Questionnaire* (Technical Report). Berlin: Max Planck Institute for Human Development and Education.

Heckhausen, J. (1992). *Life course patterns, developmental projects, and control beliefs in East- and West-Berliners born between 1920 and 1970: A study outline.* Unpublished manuscript, Max Planck Institute for Human Development and Education, Berlin, Germany.

Heckhausen, J. (1993, April). *An analysis of "good" stress and coping in adulthood and old age.* In E. Skinner (Chair). *The search for "good" stress and coping: An analysis of developmentally adaptive stress across the life span.* Symposium presented at the 60th meeting of the Society for Research in Child Development, New Orleans.

Heckhausen, J., & Krueger, J. (1993). Developmental expectations for the self and "most other people": Age grading in three functions of social comparison. *Developmental Psychology, 29*, 539-548.

Heckhausen, J., & Schulz, R. (in press). A life-span theory of control. *Psychological Review.*

Heyman, G. D., Dweck, C. S., & Cain, K. M. (1992). Young children's vulnerability to self-blame and helplessness: Relationship to beliefs about goodness. *Child Development, 63*, 401-415.

Hoff, E., & Hohner, H. (1986). Occupational careers, work, and control. In M. M. Baltes & P. B. Baltes (Eds.), *The psychology of control and aging* (pp. 345-371). Hillsdale, NJ: Lawrence Erlbaum.

Hymel, S., Bowker, A., & Woody, E. (1993). Aggressive versus withdrawn unpopular children: Variations in peer and self-perceptions in multiple domains. *Child Development, 64*, 879-896.

Hymel, S., & Franke, S. (1985). Children's peer relations: Assessing self-perceptions. In B. H. Schneider, K. H. Rubin, & J. E. Ledingham (Eds.), *Children's peer relations: Issues in assessment and intervention* (pp. 75-92). New York: Springer.

Janoff-Bulman, R. (1979). Characterological versus behavioral self-blame: Inquiries into depression and rape. *Journal of Personality and Social Psychology, 37*, 1798-1809.

Janoff-Bulman, R., & Brickman, P. (1982). Expectations and what people learn from failure. In N. T. Feather (Eds.), *Expectations and actions: Expectancy-value models in psychology* (pp. 207-237). Hillsdale, NJ: Lawrence Erlbaum.

Janos, O., & Papousek, H. (1977). Acquisition of appetitional and palpebral conditioned reflexes by the same infants. *Early Human Development, 1*, 91-97.

Kaplan, R. M. (1991). Health-related quality of life in patient decision making. *Journal of Social Issues, 47*(4), 69-90.

Karuza, J., Jr., Rabinowitz, V. C., & Zevon, M. A. (1986). Implications of control and responsibility on helping the aged. In M. M. Baltes & P. B. Baltes (Eds.), *The psychology of control and aging* (pp. 373-396). Hillsdale, NJ: Lawrence Erlbaum.

Kiecolt-Glaser, J. K., & Glaser, R. (1990). Behavioral influences on immune function: Evidence for the interplay between stress and health. In T. Field, P. McCade, & A. Schneiderman (Eds.), *Stress and coping* (pp. 189-206). Hillsdale, NJ: Lawrence Erlbaum.

Koestner, R., & McClelland, D. C. (1990). Perspectives on competence motivation. In L. A. Pervin (Ed.), *Handbook of personality: Theory and research* (pp. 527-548). New York: Guilford.

Kofta, M., & Sedek, G. (1989). Learned helplessness: Affective or cognitive disturbance? In C. D. Spielberger, I. G. Sarason, & J. Strelau (Eds.), *Stress and anxiety* (pp. 81-96). Washington, DC: Hemisphere.

Kopp, C. (1982). Antecedents of self-regulation: A developmental perspective. *Developmental Psychology, 18*(2), 199-214.

Krampen, G. (1987). Entwicklung von kontrollüberzeugungen: Thesen zu forschungsstand und perspektiven (*The development of control beliefs: Propositions for current research and future perspectives*). *Zeitschrift für Entwicklungspsychologie und Padagogische Psychologie, 19,* 195-227.

Krampen, G. (1989). Perceived childrearing practices and the development of locus of control in early adolescence. *International Journal of Behavioral Development, 12*(2), 177-193.

Kuhl, J. (1981). Motivational and functional helplessness: The moderating effect of state versus action orientation. *Journal of Personality and Social Psychology, 40*(1), 155-170.

Kuhl, J. (1984). Volitional aspects of achievement motivation and learned helplessness: Toward a comprehensive theory of action control. In B. A. Maber (Ed.), *Progress in experimental personality research* (pp. 99-171). New York: Academic Press.

Kuhl, J. (1986). Aging and models of control: The hidden costs of wisdom. In M. M. Baltes & P. B. Baltes (Eds.), *The psychology of control and aging* (pp. 1-33). Hillsdale, NJ: Lawrence Erlbaum.

Kurdek, L. A., & Krile, D. (1982). A developmental analysis of the relation between peer acceptance and both interpersonal understanding and perceived social self-competence. *Child Development, 53,* 1485-1491.

Kurtz, B. E., & Burkowski, J. G. (1984). Children's metacognition: Exploring relations between knowledge, process, and motivational variables. *Journal of Experimental Child Psychology, 37,* 335-354.

Lachman, M. E. (1986a). Locus of control in aging research: A case for multidimensional and domain-specific assessment. *Psychology and Aging, 1,* 34-40.

Lachman, M. E. (1986b). Personal control in later life: Stability, change, and cognitive correlates. In M. M. Baltes & P. B. Baltes (Eds.), *The psychology of control and aging* (pp. 207-236). Hillsdale, NJ: Lawrence Erlbaum.

Lachman, M. E. (1991). Perceived control over memory aging: Developmental and intervention perspectives. *Journal of Social Issues, 47*(4), 159-175.

Lachman, M. E., & Burack, O. R. (1993). Planning and control processes across the life span: An overview. *International Journal of Behavioral Development, 16*(2), 131-143.

Ladd, G. W., & Crick, N. R. (1989). Probing the psychological environment: Children's cognitions, perceptions, and feelings in the peer culture. In C. Ames &

M. Maehr (Eds.), *Advances in motivation and achievement* (Vol. 6, pp. 1-44). Greenwich, CT: JAI Press.

Lamb, M. E., & Easterbrooks, M. A. (1981). Individual differences in parental sensitivity: Some thoughts about origins, components, and consequences. In M. E. Lamb & L. R. Sherrod (Eds.), *Infant social cognition: Empirical and theoretical considerations* (pp. 127-153). Hillsdale, NJ: Lawrence Erlbaum.

Langer, E. J., & Rodin, J. (1976). The effects of choice and enhanced personal responsibility for the aged: A field experiment in an institutional setting. *Journal of Personality and Social Psychology, 34,* 191-198.

Lazarus, R. S., & Folkman, S. (1984). *Stress, appraisal, and coping.* New York: Springer.

Lefcourt, H. M. (Ed.). (1981). *Research with the locus of control construct: Vol. 1. Assessment methods.* New York: Academic Press.

Lefcourt, H. M. (1982). *Locus of control: Current trends in theory and research.* New York: John Wiley.

Lefcourt, H. M. (Ed.). (1983). *Research with the locus of control construct: Vol. 2. Developments and social problems.* New York: Academic Press.

Lefcourt, H. M. (1992). Durability and impact of the locus of control construct. *Psychological Bulletin, 112*(3), 411-414.

Levenson, H. (1973). Perceived parental antecedents of internal, powerful others, and chance locus of control orientations. *Developmental Psychology, 9,* 260-265.

Levine, S. (1983). A psychobiological approach to the study of coping. In N. Garmezy & M. Rutter (Eds.), *Stress, coping and development in children* (pp. 107-131). New York: Plenum.

Lewis, M., & Brooks-Gunn, J. (1979). *Social cognition and the acquisition of self.* New York: Plenum.

Lewis, M., & Goldberg, S. (1969). Perceptual cognitive development in infancy: A generalized expectancy model as a function of mother-infant interactions. *Merrill-Palmer Quarterly, 19,* 81-100.

Little, T. D, Oettingen, G., Stetsenko, A., & Baltes, P. B. (1994a). *Children's action-related beliefs about school performance: How do American children compare to German and Russian children?* Unpublished manuscript, Max Planck Institute for Human Development and Education, Berlin, Germany.

Little, T. D, Oettingen, G., Stetsenko, A., & Baltes, P. B. (1994b). *A mean and covariance structures (MACS) assessment of the factorial structure of the Control, Agency, and Means-Ends Interview (CAMI): A cross-sample validation* (ACCD Tech. Rep. No. 1). Max Planck Institute for Human Development and Education, Berlin, Germany.

Maccoby, E. E. (1983). Social-emotional development and response to stressors. In N. Garmezy & M. Rutter (Eds.), *Stress, coping and development in children* (pp. 217-234). New York: Plenum.

Markus, H. J., & Nurius, P. S. (1984). Self-understanding and self-regulation in middle childhood. In W. A. Collins (Ed.), *Development during middle childhood: The years from six to twelve* (pp. 147-183). Washington, DC: National Academy Press.

Markus, H. R., & Kitayama, S. (1991). Culture and the self: Implications for cognition, emotion, and motivation. *Psychological Review, 98*(2), 224-253.

Masten, A. S. (1994). Resilience in development: Successful adaptation despite risk and adversity. In M. Wang & E. Gordon (Eds.), *Risk and resilience in inner city America: Challenges and prospects.* Hillsdale, NJ: Lawrence Erlbaum.

Meyer, J. W. (1990). Individualism: Social experience and cultural formulation. In J. Rodin, C. Schooler, & K. W. Schaie (Eds.), *Self-directedness: Cause and effects throughout the life course* (pp. 51-58). Hillsdale, NJ: Lawrence Erlbaum.

Millar, W. S., & Watson, J. S. (1979). The effect of delayed feedback on infant learning reexamined. *Child Development, 50,* 747-751.

Miller, A. (1985). A developmental study of the cognitive basis of performance impairment after failure. *Journal of Personality and Social Psychology, 49,* 529-538.

Miller, S. M. (1979). Controllability and human stress: Method, evidence and theory. *Behavior Research and Theory, 17,* 287-304.

Moos, R. H., & Billings, A. G. (1982). Conceptualizing and measuring coping resources and coping processes. In L. Goldberger & S. Breznitz (Eds.), *Handbook of stress: Theoretical and clinical aspects* (pp. 212-230). New York: Free Press.

Morgan, G. A., & Harmon, R. A. (1984). Developmental transformations in mastery motivation: Measurement and validation. In R. N. Emde & R. J. Harmon (Eds.), *Continuities and discontinuities in development* (pp. 263-291). New York: Plenum.

Morgan, G. A., Harmon, R. J., & Maslin-Cole, C. A. (1990). Mastery motivation: Definition and measurement. *Early Education and Development, 1*(5), 318-339.

Murray, H. A. (1938). *Explorations in personality.* New York: Oxford University Press.

Nelson, E. A. (1990). *Perceived control and age differences: A study of adult control beliefs in three domains.* Unpublished doctoral dissertation, University of Rochester, Rochester, NY.

Newcomb, A. F., Bukowski, W. M., & Pattee, L. (1993). Children's peer relations: A meta-analytic review of popular, rejected, neglected, controversial, and average sociometric status. *Psychological Bulletin, 113*(1), 99-128.

Nicholls, J. G. (1978). The development of the concepts of effort and ability, perception of academic attainment, and the understanding that difficult tasks require more ability. *Child Development, 49,* 800-814.

Nicholls, J. G. (1984). Achievement motivation: Conceptions of ability, subjective experience, task choice, and performance. *Psychological Review, 91,* 328-346.

Nolen-Hoeksma, S., Girgus, J. S., & Seligman, M. E. P. (1986). Learned helplessness in children: A longitudinal study of depression, achievement, and explanatory style. *Journal of Personality and Social Psychology, 51,* 435-142.

Oettingen, G. (1994). Cross-cultural perspectives on self-efficacy. In A. Bandura (Ed.), *Self-efficacy in changing societies.* New York: Cambridge University Press.

Oettingen, G., Little, T. D., Lindenberger, U., & Baltes, P. B. (1994). Causality, agency, and control beliefs in East versus West Berlin children: A natural experiment on the role of context. *Journal of Personality and Social Psychology, 66,* 579-595.

Okun, M., Olding, R. W., & Cohn, C. M. G. (1990). A meta-analysis of subjective well-being interventions among elders. *Psychological Bulletin, 108,* 257-266.

Papousek, H. (1967). Experimental studies of appetitional behavior in human newborns and infants. In H. W. Stevenson, E. H. Hess, & H. C. Rheingold (Eds.), *Early behavior: Comparative and developmental approaches* (pp. 249-277). New York: John Wiley.

Papousek, H., & Papousek, M. (1979). The infant's fundamental adaptive response system in social interaction. In E. B. Thoman (Ed.), *Origins of the infant's social responsiveness*. Hillsdale, NJ: Lawrence Erlbaum.

Papousek, H., & Papousek, M. (1980). Early ontogeny of human social interaction: Its biological roots and social dimensions. In M. von Cranach, K. Foppa, W. Lepenies, & D. Ploog (Eds.), *Human ethology: Claims and limits of a new discipline*. Cambridge: Cambridge University Press.

Patrick, B. C., Skinner, E. A., & Connell, J. P. (1993). What motivates children's behavior and emotion? The joint effects of perceived control and autonomy in the academic domain. *Journal of Personality and Social Psychology, 65*(4), 781-791.

Pearlin, L. I., & Schooler, C. (1978). The structure of coping. *Journal of Health and Social Behavior, 19*, 2-21.

Peterson, C. (1980). Recognition of noncontingency. *Journal of Personality and Social Psychology, 38*, 727-734.

Peterson, C., & Seligman, M.E.P. (1984). Causal explanations as a risk factor for depression: Theory and evidence. *Psychological Review, 91*, 347-374.

Piaget, J. (1976). *The grasp of consciousness: Action and concept in the young child*. Cambridge, MA: Harvard University Press.

Piaget, J. (1978). *Success and understanding*. Cambridge, MA: Harvard University Press.

Pintrich, P. R., & Blumenfeld, P. C. (1985). Classroom experience and children's self-perceptions of ability, effort, and conduct. *Journal of Educational Psychology, 77*(6), 646-657.

Price, J. M., & Ladd, G. W. (1986). Assessment of children's friendships: Implications for social competence and social adjustment. In R. J. Prinz (Ed.), *Advances in behavioral assessment of children and families* (Vol. 2, pp. 121-149). Greenwich, CT: JAI Press.

Ramey, C. T., Starr, R. H., Pallas, J., Whitten, C. F., & Reed, V. (1975). Nutrition, response contingent stimulation and the mineral deprivation syndrome: Results of an early intervention program. *Merrill-Palmer Quarterly, 21*, 45-53.

Regan, C., & Skinner, E. (1993, March). *The role of mother and father psychological provisions on children's academic engagement*. Poster presented at the Meetings of the Society for Research in Child Development, New Orleans.

Reich, J. W., & Zautra, A. J. (1991). Experimental and measurement approaches to internal control in at-risk older adults. *Journal of Social Issues, 47*(4), 143-158.

Reid, D. (1984). Participatory control and the chronic illness adjustment process. In H. Lefcourt (Ed.), *Research with the locus of control construct: Extensions and limitations* (Vol. 3, pp. 361-389). New York: Academic Press.

Remondet, J. H., & Hansson, R. O. (1993). Job-related threats to control among older employees. *Journal of Social Issues, 47*(4), 129-141.

Rholes, W. S., Blackwell, J., Jordan, C., & Walters, C. (1980). A developmental study of learned helplessness. *Developmental Psychology, 16*, 616-624.

Riksen-Walraven, J. M. (1978). Effects of caregiver behavior on habituation rate and self-efficacy in infants. *International Journal of Behavioural Development, 1*, 105-130.

Rodin, J. (1980). Managing the stress of aging: The role of coping and control. In S. Levine & H. Ursin (Eds.), *Coping and health*. New York: Plenum.

Rodin, J. (1986). Personal control through the life course. In R. Abeles (Ed.), *Implications of the life span perspective for social psychology* (pp. 103-120). Hillsdale, NJ: Lawrence Erlbaum.

Rodin, J. (1990). Control by any other name: Definitions, concepts, and processes. In J. Rodin, C. Schooler, & K. W. Schaie (Eds.), *Self-directedness: Cause and effects throughout the life course* (pp. 1-17). Hillsdale, NJ: Lawrence Erlbaum.

Rodin, J., Rennert, K., & Solomon, S. K. (1980). Intrinsic motivation for control: Fact or fiction. In A. Baum & J. E. Singer (Eds.), *Advances in environmental psychology* (pp. 131-148). Hillsdale, NJ: Lawrence Erlbaum.

Rodin, J., Timko, C., & Harris, S. (1985). The construct of control: Biological and psychological correlates. In M. P. Lawton & G. L. Maddox (Eds.), *Annual review of gerontology and geriatrics* (pp. 3-55). New York: Springer.

Rosenholtz, S. J., & Simpson, C. (1984). The formation of ability conceptions: Developmental trend or social construction? *Review of Educational Research, 54*(1), 31-63.

Rossman, B. R., & Rosenberg, M. S. (1992). Family stress and functioning in children: The moderating effects of children's beliefs about their control over parental conflict. *Journal of Child Psychology and Psychiatry, 33*(4), 699-715.

Rothbaum, F., Weisz, J. R., & Snyder, S. S. (1982). Changing the world and changing the self: A two-process model of perceived control. *Journal of Personality and Social Psychology, 42*(1), 5-37.

Rotter, J. B. (1966). Generalized expectancies for internal versus external control of reinforcement. *Psychological Monographs, 80.*

Rotter, J. B. (1975). Some problems and misconceptions related to the construct of internal versus external control of reinforcement. *Journal of Consulting and Clinical Psychology, 43,* 56-67.

Rotter, J. B. (1990). Internal versus external control of reinforcement: A case history of a variable. *American Psychologist, 45*(4), 489-493.

Ruble, D. N., Feldman, N. S., & Boggiano, A. K. (1976). Social comparison between young children in achievement situations. *Developmental Psychology, 12,* 192-197.

Rutter, M. (1983). Stress, coping and development: Some issues and some questions. In N. Garmezy & M. Rutter (Eds.), *Stress, coping and development in children* (pp. 1-41). New York: McGraw-Hill.

Rutter, M. (1989). Pathways from childhood to adult life. *Journal of Child Psychology, 30*(1), 23-51.

Ryan, R. M. (1982). Control and information in the intrapersonal sphere: An extension of cognitive evaluation theory. *Journal of Personality and Social Psychology, 43,* 450-461.

Schmitz, B. (1987). *Zeitreihenanlyse in der Psychologie: Verfahren zur Veraenderungsmessung und Prozessdiagnostik (Time series analysis in psychology: Methods for the measurement of change and process evaluation).* Weinheim, Germany: Beltz.

Schmitz, B., & Skinner, E. (1993). Perceived control, effort, and academic performance: Interindividual, intraindividual, and multivariate time-series analyses. *Journal of Personality and Social Psychology, 64*(6), 1010-1028.

Schneider, W. (1985). Developmental trends in the metamemory-memory behavior relationship: An integrative review. In D. L. Forrest-Pressley, G. E. MacKinnon,

& T. G. Waller (Eds.), *Cognition, metacognition, and human performance*. New York: Academic Press.

Scholnick, E. K., & Friedman, S. L. (1993). Planning in context: Developmental and situational considerations. *International Journal of Behavioral Development, 16*(2), 145-167.

Schooler, C. (1990). Individualism and the historical and social-structural determinants of people's concerns over self-directedness and efficacy. In J. Rodin, C. Schooler, & K. W. Schaie (Eds.), *Self-directedness: Cause and effects throughout the life course* (pp. 19-49). Hillsdale, NJ: Lawrence Erlbaum.

Schulz, R. (1976). Effects of control and predictability on the psychological well-being of the institutionalized aged. *Journal of Personality and Social Psychology, 33*, 101-120.

Schunk, D. H. (1990). Goal-setting and self-efficacy during self-regulated learning. *Educational Psychologist, 25*, 71-86.

Schustack, M. W., & Sternberg, R. J. (1981). Evaluation of evidence in causal inference. *Journal of Experimental Psychology: General, 110*, 101-120.

Sedek, G., & Kofta, M. (1990). When cognitive exertion does not yield cognitive gain: Toward an informational explanation of learned helplessness. *Journal of Personality and Social Psychology, 58*(4), 729-743.

Seligman, M. E. P. (1975). *Helplessness: On depression, development, and death*. San Francisco: Freeman.

Shaklee, H., & Mims, M. (1981). Development of rule use in judgments of covariation between events. *Child Development, 52*, 317-325.

Shultz, T. R., Butkowsky, I., Pearce, J. W., & Shanfield, H. (1975). Development of schemes for the attribution of multiple psychological causes. *Developmental Psychology, 11*(4), 502-510.

Shultz, T. R., Fisher, G. W., Pratt, C. C., & Rulf, S. (1986). Selection of causal rules. *Child Development, 57*, 143-152.

Skinner, E. A. (1985a). Action, control judgments, and the structure of control experience. *Psychological Review, 92*, 39-58.

Skinner, E. A. (1985b). Determinants of mother sensitive and contingent-responsive behavior: The role of child-rearing beliefs and socioeconomic status. In I. Siegel (Ed.), *The role of parental belief systems as influences on parent-child interactions* (pp. 51-82). Hillsdale, NJ: Lawrence Erlbaum.

Skinner, E. A. (1986). The origins of young children's perceived control: Caregiver contingent and sensitive behavior. *International Journal of Behavioral Development, 9*, 359-382.

Skinner, E. A. (1987, December). *Perceived control and friendship: Development during middle childhood*. Paper presented at the Workshop on Beliefs About the Life Span: Developmental Change and Behavioral Consequences, Max Planck Institute for Human Development and Education, Berlin, West Germany.

Skinner, E. A. (1990a). Age differences in the dimensions of perceived control during middle childhood: Implications for developmental conceptualizations and research. *Child Development, 61*, 1882-1890.

Skinner, E. A. (1990b). What causes success and failure in school and friendship? Developmental differentiation of children's beliefs across middle childhood. *International Journal of Behavioral Development, 13*, 157-176.

Skinner, E. A. (1991a). Development and perceived control: A dynamic model of action in context. In M. Gunnar & L. A. Sroufe (Eds.), *Minnesota Symposium on Child Psychology* (pp. 167-216). Chicago: University of Chicago Press.

Skinner, E. A. (1991b, April). *Peer relations and the self-system.* Presentation at the Preconference on Peer Relationships at the Meetings of the Society for Research in Child Development, Seattle.

Skinner, E. A. (1992). Perceived control: Motivation, coping, and development. In R. Schwarzer (Ed.), *Self-efficacy: Thought control of action* (pp. 91-106). London: Hemisphere Publishing.

Skinner, E. A. (1994). *Is more control better? A simple answer to a complex question.* Unpublished manuscript, Portland State University, Portland, OR.

Skinner, E. A. (in press). Planning and perceived control. In S. Friedman & E. Scholnick (Eds.), *Why, how, and when do we plan? The developmental psychology of planning.* Hillsdale, NJ: Lawrence Erlbaum.

Skinner, E. A., Altman, J., & Sherwood, H. (1991). *Coding manual for children's coping in the domains of school and friendship.* Technical report, University of Rochester, Rochester, NY.

Skinner, E. A., Altman, J., & Sherwood, H. (1993). *An analysis of open-ended interviews of children's coping in the domains of academics and friendship.* Unpublished manuscript, University of Rochester, Rochester, NY.

Skinner, E. A., Altman, J., Sherwood, H., Yoder, R., & Grossmann, S. J. (1994). *A catalog of coping categories.* Unpublished manuscript, Portland State University, Portland, OR.

Skinner, E. A., & Belmont, M. J. (1993). Motivation in the classroom: Reciprocal effects of teacher behavior and student engagement across the school year. *Journal of Educational Psychology, 85,* 571-581.

Skinner, E. A., & Chapman, M. (1987). One resolution of a developmental paradox: How can perceived internality increase, decrease, and remain the same across middle childhood? *Developmental Psychology, 23,* 44-48.

Skinner, E. A., Chapman, M., & Baltes, P. B. (1983). *The Control, Agency and Means-ends Interview (CAMI)* (English and German versions) (Technical Report). Berlin: Max Planck Institute for Human Development and Education.

Skinner, E. A., Chapman, M., & Baltes, P. B. (1988a). Beliefs about control, means-ends, and agency: Developmental differences during middle childhood. *International Journal of Behavioral Development, 11,* 369-388.

Skinner, E. A., Chapman, M., & Baltes, P. B. (1988b). Control, means-ends, and agency beliefs: A new conceptualization and its measurement during childhood. *Journal of Personality and Social Psychology, 54,* 117-133.

Skinner, E. A., & Connell, J. P. (1986). Control understanding: Suggestions for a developmental framework. In M. M. Baltes & P. B. Baltes (Eds.), *The psychology of control and aging* (pp. 35-69). Hillsdale, NJ: Lawrence Erlbaum.

Skinner, E. A., & Regan, C. (1991). *The Parents as Social Context Questionnaire (PASCQ): Parent and child reports of parent involvement, structure, and autonomy support.* Technical report, University of Rochester, Rochester, NY.

Skinner, E. A., & Schmitz, B. (1994). *Intraindividual analysis of the causes of attributions: Covariation or beliefs?* Unpublished manuscript, Portland State University, Portland, OR.

Skinner, E. A., & Wellborn, J. G. (1992). *Children's coping in the academic domain.* Technical report, University of Rochester, Rochester, NY.

Skinner, E. A., & Wellborn, J. G. (1994). Coping during childhood and adolescence: A motivational perspective. In D. Featherman, R. Lerner, & M. Perlmutter (Eds.), *Life-span development and behavior* (pp. 91-133). Hillsdale, NJ: Lawrence Erlbaum.

Skinner, E. A., Wellborn, J. G., & Connell, J. P. (1990). What it takes to do well in school and whether I've got it: The role of perceived control in children's engagement and school achievement. *Journal of Educational Psychology, 82,* 22-32.

Skinner, E. A., Zimmer-Gembeck, M., & Connell, J. P. (1994). *A longitudinal study of children's beliefs about strategies and capacities for control: A model of context, self, and action.* Manuscript in preparation, Portland State University, Portland, OR.

Sroufe, L. A. (1979). The coherence of individual development: Early care attachment and subsequent developmental issues. *American Psychologist, 34,* 834-841.

Steitz, J. A. (1982). Locus of control as a life-span developmental process: Revision of the construct. *International Journal of Behavioral Development, 5,* 299-316.

Stetsenko, A., Little, T. D., Oettingen, G., & Baltes, P. B. (in press). Agency, control, and means-ends beliefs about school performance in Moscow children: How similar are they to beliefs of Western children? *Developmental Psychology.*

Stipek, D. (1980). A causal analysis of the relationship between locus of control and academic achievement in first grade. *Contemporary Educational Psychology, 5,* 90-99.

Stipek, D. J. (1984). Young children's performance expectations: Logical analysis or wishful thinking? In M. Haehr (Ed.), *Advances in motivation and achievement* (pp. 33-56). Greenwich, CT: JAI Press.

Stipek, D. J., & Weisz, J. R. (1981). Perceived personal control and academic achievement. *Review of Educational Research, 51,* 101-137.

Strickland, B. R. (1989). Internal-external control expectancies: From contingency to creativity. *American Psychologist, 44*(1), 1-12.

Taylor, S. E. (1979). Hospital patient behavior: Reactance, helplessness, or control? *Journal of Social Issues, 35*(1), 156-184.

Taylor, S. E. (1983). Adjustment to threatening events: A theory of cognitive adaptation. *American Psychologist, 38,* 1161-1173.

Taylor, S. E. (1989). *Positive illusions: Creative self-deception and the healthy mind.* New York: Basic Books.

Taylor, S. E., Helgeson, V. S., Reed, G. M., & Skokan, L. A. (1991). Self-generated feelings of control and adjustment to physical illness. *Journal of Social Issues, 47*(4), 91-109.

Taylor, S., & Brown, J. (1988). Illusion and well-being: A social psychological perspective on mental health. *Psychological Bulletin, 103,* 193-210.

Tennen, H., Drum, P., Gillen, R., & Stanton, A. (1982). Learned helplessness and the detection of contingency: A direct test. *Journal of Personality, 50*(4), 426-442.

Thompson, S. C. (1981). Will it hurt less if I can control it? A complex answer to a simple question. *Psychological Bulletin, 90*(1), 89-101.

Thompson, S. C., Sobolew-Shubin, A., Galbraith, M. E., Schwankowsky, L., & Cruzen, D. (1993). Maintaining perceptions of control: Finding perceived control in low-control circumstances. *Journal of Personality and Social Psychology, 64*(2), 293-304.

Thompson, S. C., & Spacapan, S. (1991). Perceptions of control in vulnerable populations. *Journal of Social Issues, 47*(4), 1-21.

Vroom, V. H. (1964). *Work and motivation.* New York: John Wiley.

Wallston, K. A. (1992). Hocus-pocus, the focus isn't strictly on locus: Rotter's social learning theory modified for health. *Cognitive Therapy and Research, 16*(2), 183-199.

Wannon, M. (1990). *Children's control attributions about controllable and uncontrollable events: Their relationship to stress-resiliency and psychosocial adjustment.* Unpublished doctoral dissertation, University of Rochester, New York.

Watson, J. S. (1966). The development and generalization of "contingency awareness" in early infancy: Some hypotheses. *Merrill-Palmer Quarterly, 12,* 123-135.

Watson, J. S. (1971). Cognitive-perceptual development in infancy: Setting for the seventies. *Merrill-Palmer Quarterly, 17,* 139-152.

Watson, J. S. (1979). Perception of contingency as a determinant of social responsiveness. In E. B. Thoman (Ed.), *The origins of the infant's social responsiveness.* Hillsdale, NJ: Lawrence Erlbaum.

Watson, M., Greer, S., Pruyn, J., & van den Borne, B. (1990). Locus of control and adjustment to cancer. *Psychological Reports, 66,* 39-48.

Weigel, C., Wertlieb, D., & Feldstein, M. (1989). Perceptions of control, competence, and contingency as influences on the stress-behavior symptom relation in school-age children. *Journal of Personality and Social Psychology, 56*(3), 456-464.

Weinberg, J., & Levine, S. (1980). Psychobiology of coping in animals: The effects of predictability. In S. Levine & H. Ursin (Eds.), *Coping and health* (pp. 39-59). New York: Plenum.

Weiner, B. (1985a). An attributional theory of achievement motivation and emotion. *Psychological Review, 92,* 548-573.

Weiner, B. (1985b). "Spontaneous" causal thinking. *Psychological Bulletin, 97,* 74-84.

Weiner, B. (1986). *An attributional theory of motivation and emotion.* New York: Springer.

Weiner, B., Kun, A., & Benesh-Weiner, M. (1980). The development of mastery, emotions, and morality from an attributional perspective. In A. Collins (Ed.), *Minnesota Symposium on Child Psychology* (Vol. 13). Hillsdale, NJ: Lawrence Erlbaum.

Weiner, B., Nierenberg, R., & Goldstein, M. (1976). Social learning (locus of control) versus attributional (causal stability) interpretations of expectancy of success. *Journal of Personality, 44,* 52-68.

Weisz, J. R. (1983). Can I control it? The pursuit of veridical answers across the life span. In P. B. Baltes & O. G. Brim, Jr. (Eds.), *Life-span development and behavior* (pp. 233-300). New York: Academic Press.

Weisz, J. R. (1986). Understanding the developing understanding of control. In M. Perlmutter (Ed.), *Social cognition: Minnesota Symposia on Child Psychology* (Vol. 18, pp. 219-278). Hillsdale, NJ: Lawrence Erlbaum.

Weisz, J. R., & Stipek, D. J. (1982). Competence, contingency, and the development of perceived control. *Human Development, 25,* 250-281.

Wellborn, J. G. (1991). *Engaged and disaffected action: The conceptualization and measurement of motivation in the academic domain.* Unpublished doctoral dissertation, University of Rochester, New York.

Wellborn, J. G. (1993). *Parents as sources of support: A motivational perspective on parental social support and academic coping in early adolescence.* Unpublished manuscript, Vanderbilt University, Nashville, TN.

Wellborn, J. G., Connell, J. P., & Skinner, E. A. (1988). *The Student's Perceptions of Control Questionnaire (SPOCQ): Academic domain.* Technical report, University of Rochester, New York.

Wellborn, J., Connell, J., Skinner, E. A., & Pierson, L. H. (1988). *Teacher as social context: A measure of teacher provision of involvement, structure, and autonomy support.* Technical report, University of Rochester, New York.

Wheeler, V. A., & Ladd, G. W. (1982). Assessment of children's self-efficacy for social interactions with peers. *Developmental Psychology, 18,* 795-805.

White, C. B., & Janson, P. (1986). Helplessness in institutional settings: Adaptation or iatrogenic disease? In M. M. Baltes & P. B. Baltes (Eds.), *The psychology of control and aging* (pp. 297-314). Hillsdale, NJ: Lawrence Erlbaum.

White, P. A. (1988). Causal processing: Origins and development. *Psychological Bulletin, 104*(1), 36-52.

White, R. W. (1959). Motivation reconsidered: The concept of competence. *Psychological Review, 66,* 297-333.

Wigfield, A., Eccles, J. S., MacIver, D., Reuman, D. A., & Midgley, C. (1991). Transitions during early adolescence: Changes in children's domain-specific self-perceptions and general self-esteem across the transition to junior high school. *Developmental Psychology, 27*(4), 552-565.

Wood, D. (1980). Teaching the young child: Some relationships between social interaction, language, and thought. In D. Olson (Ed.), *The social foundations of language and thought* (pp. 280-296). New York: Norton.

Wortman, C. B., & Brehm, J. W. (1975). Responses to uncontrollable outcomes: An integration of reactance theory and the learned helplessness model. In L. Berkowitz (Ed.), *Advances in experimental social psychology* (pp. 277-336). New York: Academic Press.

# Author Index

# Subject Index

209

# About the Author

**Ellen A. Skinner** was trained as a life-span developmental psychologist at the Pennsylvania State University, from which she received a Ph.D. in Human Development in 1981. She spent the next 7 years as a Research Scientist at the Max Planck Institute for Human Development and Education in Berlin, Germany. In 1988 she joined the faculty at the University of Rochester to work with the Motivation Research Group. In fall 1992 she moved to Portland State University. She has conducted research and written about the development of the self and perceived control, and the parent and school contexts that promote and undermine them. Her work has been generously supported by the Foundation for Child Development, the Max Planck Institute, the William T. Grant Foundation, and research and training grants from the National Institute of Mental Health and the National Institute of Child Health and Human Development.